DATE DUE

A JEWISH CHAPLAIN IN
FRANCE

THE MACMILLAN COMPANY
NEW YORK · BOSTON · CHICAGO · DALLAS
ATLANTA · SAN FRANCISCO

MACMILLAN & CO., LIMITED
LONDON · BOMBAY · CALCUTTA
MELBOURNE

THE MACMILLAN CO. OF CANADA, LTD.
TORONTO

A group of Jewish welfare workers at Le Mans, France, in March, 1919. From left to right, George Rooby, Julius Halperin, Frank M. Dart, Chaplain Lee J. Levinger, Adele Winston, Charles S. Rivitz, David Rosenthal and Esther Levy.

A Jewish Chaplain in France

BY

RABBI LEE J. LEVINGER, M.A.,

**Executive Director Young Men's Hebrew Association, New York City,
formerly First Lieutenant Chaplain United States Army**

WITH A FOREWORD BY

CYRUS ADLER, Ph.D.,

President of Dropsie College for Hebrew and Cognate Learning, Philadelphia

New York
THE MACMILLAN COMPANY
1922

TO A GOOD SOLDIER
WHO SENT ME TO FRANCE
AND BROUGHT ME BACK AGAIN·
MY WIFE

FOREWORD

The tendency to "forget the war" is not admirable. Such an attitude is in effect a negation of thought. The agony which shook mankind for more than four years and whose aftermath will be with us in years to come cannot be forgotten unless the conscience of mankind is dead. Rabbi Levinger's book is the narrative of a man who saw this great tragedy, took a part in it and has thought about it.

In all the wars of the United States Jews participated, increasingly as their numbers grew appreciably. They served both as officers and privates from Colonial days. But not until the World War was a Rabbi appointed a Chaplain in the United States Army or Navy for actual service with the fighting forces. President Lincoln appointed several Jewish ministers of religion as chaplains to visit the wounded in the hospitals, but the tradition of the Army up to the period of the Great War, rendered the appointment of a Rabbi as chaplain impossible. The chaplain had been a regimental officer and was always either a Protestant or a Catholic. The sect was determined by the majority of the regiment. When the United States entered the Great War, this was clearly brought out and it required an Act of Congress to render possible the appointment of chaplains of the faiths not then represented in the body of chaplains. Twenty chaplains were thus authorized of whom six were allotted to the Synagogue the remainder being distributed among the Unitarians, who were not included in the Evangelical Churches, and the other smaller Christian sects which had grown up in America.

In order to meet the requirements of the War Department and in consonance with the spirit of unity which the war engendered, it was necessary for the Jewish organizations to create a body which could sift the applications for chaplaincies and certify them to the War Department, as being proper persons and meeting the requirements of the law of being regularly ordained ministers of religion.

Judaism in America is far from being a united body. Its differences may not be such as rise to the dignity of separate sects but they are considerable in belief and even more pronounced in practice. Membership in the various Rabbinical and synagogue organizations is voluntary and each synagogue is autonomous. In the face of the awfulness of the war, these differences seemed minimized and through the coöperation of all the Rabbinical associations and synagogue organizations, a Committee was created under the general authority of the Jewish Welfare Board which examined the credentials of all Jewish candidates for chaplaincies and made recommendations to the War Department. So conscientiously did this Committee perform its duties that every Rabbi recommended as a chaplain was commissioned.

As the law exempted ministers of religion and

theological students, no person could be drafted for a chaplaincy. Every clergyman who served was a volunteer. It is therefore greatly to the credit of the Jewish ministry in America that one-hundred and forty men volunteered for the service. As there are probably less than four hundred English speaking Rabbis in the United States, many of whom would have been disqualified by the age limit and some by their country of origin, the response of the American Rabbinate to this call, is a most gratifying evidence of their patriotism and of their sense of public service.

Rabbi Levinger's narrative is his own, in the main and properly enough a personal one, but it is representative of the work of some thirty men some of whom ministered to the troops who did not go abroad whilst others had the opportunity of being in the midst of the Great Adventure. Every one who saw the troops overseas, could not doubt the real service of the chaplain or the appeal that religion made to the men in uniform. However the armchair philosophers may have viewed the war, it strengthened the faith of the men who were engaged; hundreds of thousands of young men turned to the chaplain who would have been indifferent to him at home. That this was true of Jewish young men is certain and if there has been a reaction on the part of these young men who returned from the war, let it be blamed not so much upon religion, as upon the disappointment in the soldiers' minds at the attitude of the millions of their fellow citizens who remained at home and who want to "forget the war." The soldier who came back and found that his fellow citizens had their nerves so over-wrought by reading of the war in newspapers that they immediately entered upon a period of wild extravagances and wilder pleasure, might very well have had his faith, newly acquired if you choose, shaken by this evident lack of seriousness on the part of his fellow countrymen.

I shall not commend Rabbi Levinger's book to his readers, because if the book does not commend itself, no approbation will. As an officer of the Jewish Welfare Board whose purpose was to join with other organizations in contributing to the welfare of the American soldiers and sailors and particularly to provide for the religious needs of those of the Jewish faith, I want to express the obligations of the Board to the Rabbis who without experience or previous training for the purpose, entered upon this service and carried it through with distinction. Had it not been for them, the overseas work of the Board would have been comparatively limited and many a Jewish boy would have been deprived of the comforts and solace of his religion.

I cannot help but think that the chaplain himself derived much benefit from his service. In sections of the synagogue, as I believe in sections of the church, men are on many occasions a minority in the congregation and ministration is largely to women and children. It meant something for the chaplain to have great congregations of men, and of young men at that, and I am inclined to think hardened his mental and even spiritual fiber. It emphasized too the importance of emotion and sentiment as against mere rationalism. The worship meant more than a preachment, and sympathetic human contact for a minute was worth a barrel of oratory.

The fine spirit of liberality which grew up among the chaplains of the various faiths, reflecting as it did the comradeship of the men themselves, should not and will not be lost. The brotherhood of man will be a mere abstraction until individual men can act as brothers to one another. The ministers of religion, if they have any God-given mission above all others, surely have that of leading men, however different their physical and spiritual equipment, into the bonds of a common brotherhood. By this way and this way alone will mankind arrive at lasting peace.

CYRUS ADLER.

October 19, 1921.

PREFACE

This book is the result of the profound conviction that we are forgetting or ignoring the lessons of the World War to Israel, America and humanity. During the war such words as morale, democracy, Americanism, became a sort of cant—so much so that their actual content was forgotten. Now that the war is over and their constant repetition is discontinued, the grave danger exists that we may lose their very real influence.

These personal experiences and conclusions worked out by an army chaplain as a result of his overseas service may have some historical value also, especially as the same ground has not yet been covered by any Jewish chaplain or welfare worker in the American Expeditionary Forces. The rôle played by Jews in the army and navy of the United States and the Jewish contribution to the morale of the forces overseas deserve preservation, both as a reminder to ourselves and to the nation.

When the possibility of this book was first discussed in Paris with the late Colonel Harry Cutler, Chairman of the Jewish Welfare Board, he spoke of writing a foreword for it. Since his lamented death, Dr. Cyrus Adler, his successor as acting Chairman, has consented to fulfill the same friendly task. In addition to Dr. Adler, I acknowledge my great indebtedness to Mr. Harry L. Glucksman, Executive Director of the Jewish Welfare Board, for

PREFACE

giving me full access to their records; to Mr. John Goldhaar for his personal reminiscences of the welfare work overseas; to Captain Elkan C. Voorsanger for the invaluable suggestions based upon his vast personal experiences; to Justice Irving Lehman, President of the Young Men's Hebrew Association, for his encouragement and friendly advice; to a host of coworkers and friends in both France and America for the brilliant deeds and cordial comradeship which are here embodied; and finally to my secretary, Miss Hattie Tanzer, for her invaluable assistance in seeing the book through the press.

Much of the material used here has already been published in the form of articles appearing at various times in the *American Hebrew, American Israelite, Biblical World, B'nai B'rith News, Hebrew Standard, Jewish Forum* and *Reform Advocate*.

LEE J. LEVINGER.

New York, May, 1921.

CONTENTS

CHAPTER I

IN giving the story and the opinions of a Jewish chaplain in the American Expeditionary Forces, some statement is necessary of the work of the chaplains as a whole. Chaplains are an essential part of the organization of a modern army and it is notable that General Pershing repeatedly requested that the number of chaplains be doubled in the forces under his command. Hardly a narrative of soldiers' experiences exists without due place being given to the chaplain. In every army in France, chaplains were frequently cited for heroism and in innumerable instances suffered and died with the men in the ranks.

There are two popular impressions of the purpose of the chaplain in the military service; the one sees him as a survival of mediævalism, blessing the weapons of the men at arms; the other welcomes him as a faint harbinger of a dawning humanitarianism, one of the few men in an army who does not have to kill, but is there to save. Some people think of the physician and chaplain as having non-military work to do, as being a kind of concession to the pacific spirit of our generation.

The actual work of the chaplain is quite as unknown to the general public. People wonder what he does between weekly sermons, much as they won-

1

der what the minister or rabbi does during the six
and a half days a week that he is not preaching. In
fact, I have been greeted with frank or hidden in-
credulity whenever I admitted that in the army I
used to preach up to fifteen times a week, but never
had time to write a sermon. People wonder sometimes whether the soldiers and sailors can bear so
much preaching, sometimes what else they demand
of the chaplain. In fact, to the non-military mind
the whole subject seems shrouded in mystery.

To the military man the subject is extremely
simple. There is no mystery about it. The chaplain is in the army as the physician is, as the thousands of other non-combatants are, for a strictly
military purpose. It happens that the non-combatants may use non-military methods. One may
drive a locomotive, another carry a stretcher, another sit in an office and make out papers. All are
essential to the military machine; none is in the service for any special humanitarian purpose; none is
present as a survival of mediævalism, but all to take
part in the grim conflict of the twentieth century.
The work of a physician in the military service is
the very utilitarian one of saving men's lives and
returning them to the front. The work of a chaplain is the equally essential and practical one of
stimulating the morale of the troops.

Many factors bear upon the morale of a body of
men,—their physical environment, the strength and
spirit of their individual units, the temper and ability of their leaders. In our army we were very
fortunate in the activity of various civilian organizations which labored among the men in the service with the backing of our entire citizenry, or at

least of large and influential groups. The home service of the Red Cross and other non-military organizations was of great importance in keeping up the morale of the families left behind and through them of the men overseas. These important organizations, however, were under the handicap of doing civilian work among soldiers—a handicap whose seriousness only a soldier himself can ever realize. Some months after the war was over, the army recognized its obligation by appointing morale officers for both larger and smaller units, with others under them to supervise athletics, entertainment, and the like. The civilian organizations then conducted their activities under the orders of the morale officer.

But nearest of all to the men, because themselves a part of the actual military machine, were their own chaplains. The chaplain was under the same orders as the men, took the same risk, wore the same uniform, and naturally was regarded in every way as one of their own. I have even heard old army men scorning the new advances of all these new wartime societies. "We have our own chaplain," they said, "He looks after us all right."

The chaplain was first the religious guide of his men. He knew how to talk to them, for talking, not preaching, was the usual tone of the army or navy chaplain. He knew how to speak their own "lingo," slang and all. He knew the spiritual appeal which was most needed by these boys, transplanted, with all their boyishness, into the deep realities which few men have had to face. He knew their boyish shyness of emotion, but with it their deep, immediate need of such emotions as the love of home and God, to sustain them amid dangerous hours of duty and tempting hours of idleness. This religious need alone would have been enough work for the chaplain, even with the intended increase in numbers to three per regiment, or one chaplain for every twelve hundred men. The need for religion was evident in the training camp, the hospital, the transport, the trenches; it was evident everywhere, and the chaplain must be everywhere to satisfy it.

But in addition the chaplain had much welfare work of a more general kind to transact in connection with the various welfare agencies. One man wanted advice about getting married before leaving for the front; another had trouble at home and desired a furlough; another found himself misplaced in his work and would like a transfer. A Jewish boy came in to ask that a letter be written to his pious father; the old man had not wanted him to enlist, but would feel better if he knew there was a rabbi in the camp. Another had a request for a small service (a minyan) that he might say the memorial prayer on the anniversary of his father's death. And still another presented a letter from his home community, for he was a fine musician and wanted to help out at a concert or a "sing."

The many requests for service and the occasional offers of service made the circuit constantly from a possible teacher to a number of boys with defective English, from a potential comedy team to a crowd of eager listeners, from a timid boy with personal troubles to their remedy, either by a change in circumstances or by convincing the boy himself. Sometimes a complaint of religious prejudice had to be adjusted which might work grave harm in a company unless it were investigated and either proved groundless or remedied.

In a later chapter I shall have an opportunity to go into this more deeply. All that I want to bring out here is the important and usually misunderstood fact that American boys are restive under authority. They object vigorously to the domination of another's mind over theirs. And this objection too often took the form of bitter resentment against their officers. Therefore the final and most delicate work of the chaplain was to befriend the enlisted men against the oppression of their natural enemies and tyrants, the line officers. The army often reminds one of a school, the men are so boyish. In this régime of stringent rules which must be constantly obeyed, of short periods of intense and jovial recreation, of constant oversight by authority, the average enlisted man regarded his commanding officer much as the average small boy regards his school teacher, from whom he flees to a parent for sympathy.

That rôle of sympathetic parent was precisely the one which the chaplain was called upon to play for these boys in uniform. Not that he believed everything he was told, or took sides unfairly, or was always against authority. Simply that any boy could talk to him, as he could only to the exceptional commanding officer, and that every boy was sure that the chaplain would help him if he could. Being himself an officer, the chaplain could talk to officers more freely than any soldier could. And not being a line officer, he did not himself issue commands to any one except his own hard-worked orderly or clerk.

Thus the chaplain was fortunately placed. If he was even partially congenial, he was the one man in the army who had not an enemy high or low. The soldier looked to him for friendly aid. The officer referred to him as the great coöperating factor in building up the spirit of the troops.

During the stress of actual warfare the work of the chaplain changed in character though not in purpose. At the front the chaplain was with his boys. During a "push" he took his station at the first-aid post and worked from there as the first place to meet the wounded and dying who needed his physical or spiritual aid. He stood beside the surgeon on the battle field, he was with the stretcher-bearers searching for wounded and bringing them to safety. He rode from post to post with the ambulance driver, or tramped up to the trenches with a ration party. And wherever he went he was welcomed for his presence and for the work that he tried to do.

After a battle, when the men retired to rest and recuperate, the chaplain had to remain behind. He stayed with a group of men for the last terrible task of burying the dead. And when, that sad duty over, he returned to the troops in rest, he could not yield for a time like the others, to delicious languor after the ordeal of the battle field, hospital and ceme-tery. Then the chaplain must take up his round of duties, knowing that after the battle there is many a prayer to be said, many a hospital to be visited, many a soldier to be befriended. His task has just begun.

The military object of the chaplain is clear, to stimulate the morale of the men. But his methods were most unmilitary. Instead of reminding the men of the respect due him as an officer, the wise chaplain took his salutes as a matter of course and tried to draw the men personally, to make them forget all about military distinctions when they came to talk to him. The minute a chaplain insisted upon his rank as an officer, he lost his influence as a minister. Rank was useful to the chaplain in so far as it gave him free access to the highest authorities; it became the greatest obstacle to his work whenever the boys began to talk to him as "Lieutenant" or "Captain" instead of "Father" or "Chaplain." In the military as in the civil field the religious message can come only by personality, never by command.

The chaplain appealed for the men whenever he felt that the appeal was justified and had some chance of success, but never when it would be subversive of military discipline. He remembered always that he was in the army, a part of a great military machine, and that his presence and his work were to make the men better, not worse soldiers. He met the men personally, with their various needs and appeals, and often his best work was accomplished in short personal interviews, which would not look at all imposing on a monthly report, but which made better soldiers or happier men in one way or another. He encouraged every effort at recreation for the men, and often took part in these efforts himself. This last applies especially in the navy, where the chaplain aboard ship is the whole staff for religious, recreational, and welfare work.

In the main the work of the chaplains differed

little, whatever their religion might be. He was first of all a chaplain in the United States Army, and second a representative of his own religious body. That means that all welfare work or personal service was rendered equally to men of any faith. The only distinction authorized was between Protestant, Catholic and Jewish services, and even to these a "non-sectarian" service was often added. Wherever I went I was called upon by Jew and non-Jew alike, for in the service most men took their troubles to the nearest chaplain irrespective of his religion. The soldier discriminated only in a special case, such as the memorial prayer (kaddish) for the Jewish boy, or confession for the Catholic. The office at once insured any soldier that he had a protector and a friend.

But as there were only twelve Jewish chaplains in the entire American Expeditionary Forces, we were instructed to devote our time so far as possible to the Jewish men. At the best it was impossible for one man to fulfill the constant religious and personal needs of the thousand Jewish soldiers scattered in all the units of an entire division, as I, for one, was supposed to do. When instead of one division a Jewish chaplain was assigned several, his troubles were multiplied and his effectiveness divided. Naturally, most of the work of the Jewish chaplains had to be devoted to the needs of the Jewish soldiers, which would not otherwise be satisfied.

Any one who witnessed the labor and the self-sacrifice of chaplains of all creeds in the American army must preface an analysis of their work with a heartfelt tribute to the men themselves. I think that these men were a unique aggregation—devoted to their country and its army, yet loving men of all nations; loving each his own religion, yet rendering service to men of all creeds; bearing each his own title, yet sharing equal service and equal friendship with ministers of every other faith. I could never have accomplished one-half of the work I did without the constant friendship and hearty support of such co-workers as Father Francis A. Kelley and Rev. Almon A. Jaynes, of the 27th Division Headquarters, to mention only two notable examples among many others. I have seen Father Kelley on the battlefield going from aid post to front line trench, always most eager to be with the boys when the danger was the greatest. always cheerful, yet always a priest, doing the noble work which won him his medals and his popularity. I have seen the devotion and the regret which followed Chaplain John A. Ward of the 108th Infantry to the hospital in England after he was wounded in performance of duty, and the burst of enthusiasm which welcomed his return months afterward. I have seen one after another laboring and serving in the same spirit, and I tender to them the tribute of a co-worker who knows and admires their great accomplishments.

The place of morale in the army has not yet been studied scientifically. All that can be done as yet is to gather such personal and empirical observations as mine, which may have bearing on the general problem. These experiences were typical and these conclusions are not mine alone. They are shared by great masses, in many cases by the majority of thinking men who had like experiences. I am here setting down the most typical of the incidents which I saw or underwent and summing up the little known work of the Jewish chaplains and the Jewish Welfare Board overseas.

CHAPTER II

THE JEWISH HOLYDAYS OF 1918 IN THE A. E. F.

MY experiences as chaplain were as nearly typical as possible with any individual. A few of the Jewish chaplains saw more actual fighting than I did; a few were assigned to the Army of Occupation and saw the occupied portion of Germany. But for nine months I served as chaplain in the American Expeditionary Forces, first at the headquarters of the Intermediate Section, Service of Supply, at Nevers; then with the Twenty-Seventh Division at the front and after the armistice at the rear; finally at the American Embarkation Center at Le Mans. I worked in coöperation with the Jewish Welfare Board; I saw Paris in war time and after; I had two weeks' leave in the Riviera.

My commission as First Lieutenant Chaplain U. S. A. came to me on July 4th, 1918 at Great Lakes Naval Station, just north of Chicago, where I was then serving as Field Representative of the Jewish Welfare Board. Two weeks later I reported at Hoboken for the trip overseas. There I had the good fortune to obtain a furlough of ten days before sailing so that I was able to be back in Chicago just in time to see my new born son and daughter. I left when the babies were a week old to report back to Hoboken again for my sailing orders and found myself at sea during the tense and crucial month of August 1918.

The trip was the usual one of those anxious days
—thirteen days at sea, constant look-out for a sub-
marine, but finally a mild disappointment when we
sailed into harbor without even a scare. We carried our life preservers constantly and waited daily
for the sudden alarm of a boat drill. Our ship, the
Balmoral Castle, was one of a convoy of twelve, with
the usual quota of destroyers accompanying us.
Two days from England we met a flotilla of destroyers; later two "mystery" ships joined us and in
the Irish Sea we were greeted by a huge Blimp or
dirigible balloon. With this escort we sailed down
the Irish Sea, had a glimpse of Ireland and Scotland
and finally disembarked at Liverpool. Our first impression was the flatness of a European metropolis
when viewed at a distance and its entire lack of the
jagged sky-line of an American city.

Our pleasurable anticipations of a view of Liverpool and perhaps a glimpse of London were
rudely disappointed. We disembarked about noon,
marched through side streets, which looked like side-
streets in any of the dirtiest of American cities, lined
up at a freight station, and were loaded at once on
waiting trains and started off for Southampton.
All that afternoon we absorbed eagerly the dainty
beauty of the English countryside which most of
us knew only through literary references. We were
sorry when the late twilight shut off the view and
we had to take our first lesson at sleeping while sitting up in a train, a custom which afterward became
a habit to all officers in France.

Daybreak found us at Southampton in the rest
camp; evening on the *Maid of Orleans,* bound across
the channel. We had not seen England, we had no

place to sleep and not too much to eat, even sitting room on the decks was at a premium, but we were hastening on our way to the war. At Le Havre we were again assigned to a British rest camp, where we appreciated the contrast between the excellent meals of the officers' canteen and the primitive bunks in double tiers where we had to sleep. After two days of this sort of rest and a hasty visit to the city in between, I received orders to report to the G. H. Q. Chaplains' Office at Chaumont.

My first train journey across France impressed me at once with the unique character of the landscape. The English landscape is distinguished by meadows, the French by trees. The most realistic picture of the English landscape is the fantastic description of a checker-board in "Alice in Wonderland." In France, however, one is struck chiefly by the profusion and arrangement of trees. They are everywhere, alone or in clumps, and of all kinds, with often a formal row of poplars or a little wood of beeches to make the sky-line more impressive. In northern France the houses and barns are all of stone, peaked and windowless, with gardens that seem bent on contrasting as strongly as possible with the grayness of the walls. It seems as though tiny villages are every few feet, and always with a church steeple in the middle.

In Paris the first man I met was my old friend, Dr. H. G. Enelow, of Temple Emanu-El, New York, who was standing by the desk in the Hotel Regina when I registered. As the next day was Sunday, Dr. Enelow was able to devote some time to me, taking me for a long walk on the left bank of the Seine, where we enjoyed the gardens of the Luxem-

bourg and sipped liqueurs at a side-walk café at the
famous corner of Boulevarde St. Michel and Ger-
main. Paris in war-time was infinitely touching.
It had all the marks of the great luxury center of
the world: shops, boulevards, hotels, and show places
of every kind. But many of the most attractive of
its tiny shops were closed; the streets at night were
wrapped in the deepest gloom, with tiny shaded
lights which were not intended to illuminate but only
to show the direction of the street. The crowds
were only a little repressed in the day-time, for the
extreme crisis of the summer had just passed, but
with dusk the streets became entirely deserted.
Through Dr. Enelow I met also Dr. Jacob Kohn,
who with Dr. Enelow and Congressman Siegel constituted the commission of the Jewish Welfare
Board to outline its program for overseas work.
Dr. Enelow introduced me also to Mr. John Goldhaar, the secretary of the commission. afterward
in charge of the Paris Office of the Jewish Welfare
Board, to whom I shall refer more fully in another
connection.

At Chaumont the first man I met was my old
class-mate of the Hebrew Union College, Chaplain
Elkan C. Voorsanger, who was there temporarily detached from the 77th Division to arrange for the
celebration of the Jewish holydays throughout
France. He welcomed me, told me something of
what my work was to be, and listened to my month-
old news, which was all fresh to him. For a few
days I lingered at the chaplains' headquarters at
the old chateau of Neuilly sur Suisse, not far from
Chaumont, where thirty chaplains received their
gas mask training and instruction in front line

work, and waited for assignments. The chateau was a queer angular mediæval affair, set off by lovely lawns, with the usual rows of straight poplars all about. A few steps away was a little village with a quaint old twelfth century church, beautiful in feeling, if not in workmanship. We chaplains newly arrived in France, most of us young, and all eager to be at work, hung on the words of our leaders fresh from the line. We talked much of our ideals and our preparation, as most of the men were graduates of the Chaplains' Training School at Camp Taylor, Kentucky. My assignment came very soon to organize and conduct services for the Jewish holydays at Nevers, headquarters of the Intermediate Section, Service of Supply.

The entire American area in France had been charted out for the purpose of holyday services and the central cities designated, either those which had French synagogues to receive our men, or those points like Nevers where Americans were to be found and had to be provided for. I quote the official order which carried authority for our arrangements.

"Tours, Sept. 1, 1918.

Wherever it will not interfere with military operations soldiers of Jewish Faith will be excused from all duty and where practicable granted passes to enable them to observe Jewish Holidays as follows: from noon Sept. 6th to morning of Sept. 9th and from noon Sept. 15th to morning of Sept. 17th. If military necessity prevents granting passes on days mentioned provision should be made to hold divine services wherever possible."

This meant that all those had leave who were not

at the time in action or on the move. Chaplain
Voorsanger, for example, was not able to have any
service in the 77th Division as his troops were on
the march on New Year's Day and in action on the
Day of Atonement. Most of the central points
designated for Jewish services were important
cities with French synagogues,—Paris, Toul, Bel-
fort, Dijon, Épinal, Nantes, Rouen, Tours, Bordeaux and Marseilles. Three of the chief American
centers had none, so Dr. Enelow was assigned to
Brest, Dr. Kohn to Chaumont, and I was sent to
Nevers.

I spent a single busy day in Tours after leaving
Chaumont. I met the wife and father-in-law of
Rabbi Leon Sommers and inspected their little
synagogue with its seventy-five seats. The Rabbi
was on duty in the French army where he had been
from the very beginning of the war. I went to the
army headquarters and arranged for the proper
notices to be sent out to troops in the district, then
with two or three Jewish families whom I met I
discussed arrangements to accommodate the large
number of Jewish soldiers who would come in. I
was empowered to offer them the financial assistance of the Jewish Welfare Board in providing
such accommodations as were possible.

One surprise of a kind which I afterward came
to expect, was meeting an old friend of mine from
Great Lakes, a former sergeant in the Canadian
Army, mustered out of service because of the loss
of several fingers and now back in France again as
a representative of the Knights of Columbus.
When he left Great Lakes for overseas, I had parted
with one of the two knitted sweaters I possessed,

so that if I did not see service at least my sweater would. Now I met the sweater and its owner again for a few brief moments. These fleeting glimpses of friends became a delightful but always tense element in our army life. Men came and went like an ever-flowing stream, now and then pausing for a greeting and always hurrying on again. A single day sufficed for my work in Tours and then to my own city for the holydays.

Nevers is a historic town of thirty thousand on the banks of the River Loire. The streets are as wide as alleys and the sidewalks narrow and haphazard, so that usually one walks in the street, whether it goes up hill, down hill, or (as frequently) around the corner. But the parks and squares are frequent and lovely, and the old buildings have a charm of their own, even if it is chiefly in the quaintness of their outlines and the contrast of their gray with the sunny skies of autumn. The air was always cool and the skies always bright. I stayed at the Grand Hotel de l'Europe, a rather small place, which one had to enter by a back door through a court. With the men at war, all the work was being done by women, while most of the guests were American officers on temporary or permanent duty at the post. The cathedral (every French city seems to have one) is interesting chiefly to the antiquarian, as it has several different styles combined rather inharmoniously, and the tower is not at all imposing.

Of course, a great many Americans were stationed in or near the city—railroad engineers, training camps of combat units newly arrived in France, construction engineers, quartermaster units, and two great hospital centers. Every company I visited, every ward in the hospitals, had at least a few Jewish boys, and all of them were equally glad to see me and to attend my services. In fact, my first clear impression in France was that here lay a tremendous field for work, crying out for Jewish chaplains and other religious workers, and that we had such a pitiful force to answer the demand. At that time there were over fifty thousand Jewish soldiers in the A. E. F. at a very conservative estimate, with exactly six chaplains and four representatives of the Jewish Welfare Board to minister to them. When I took up my work at Nevers, I was simply staggered by the demands made on me and my inability to fulfill more than a fraction of them.

At first came the sudden rush of men into the city for the first day of Rosh Hashanah, the Jewish New Year. The hotels filled up almost at once; then came others who could not find accommodations, and still others who had been confined to hospitals, had drawn no pay for several months, and could not pay for a hotel room or even a shave. The problem was solved by two very helpful officers who stayed up most of the night until they had provided enough room on the barrack floors and enough blankets for all who needed them. The accommodations were crude, but the men were soldiers and glad to get them. I was doubly proud, therefore, that this crowd of ours, without official control, coming for the festival and therefore released from the incessant discipline they had become used to, never once took advantage of their privileges. We troubled the authorities for their sleeping quarters and for special permission to be on the street after nine at night—but that was all. Many of the boys may have appreciated their leave more than the festival, but all justified the confidence shown in them by their conduct.

Imagine the difference between our services in France and those to which I have been accustomed in our rather tame and formal civilian congregations. My congregation there was composed almost entirely of men, and those men all very young. We were meeting in a strange land, amid an ancient but alien civilization, which some of us liked and some disliked, but which none of us could quite understand. We had no scroll of the Law, no ram's horn, not even a complete prayer-book for the festivals. We had no synagogue, and the places we used were lent us by people of another faith, friends and co-workers, indeed, but with little interest in our festivals or our religious needs.

Our services were held in the large Y. M. C. A. hut at the chief barracks. The large, bare room was turned over to us for certain hours; the workers closed the canteen and attended the services. And in return I concluded one of the evening services fifteen minutes early so that the regular clientele would not miss their semi-weekly motion pictures. In fact, I found the Y. M. C. A. here, as everywhere, most eager to coöperate with me and to serve the Jews as well as the Christians in the army. My cantor for most of the services was Corporal Cohen of New York, although several other men volunteered for certain portions of the prayers. The head usher was Sergeant Wolf, who looked after the hall and the seating with the thoroughness characteristic of sergeants everywhere. Among the congregation were ten officers, two nurses, and three families of French Jews, as well as a mixed group of enlisted men from every branch in the army, from every section of America and every group of Jewry. The festival had caught us in a foreign land, in the service of America, and it had brought us together as nothing else could have done.

We wore our hats during the service because that was the natural desire of the majority, who were of orthodox upbringing. Of course, a soldier naturally wears his overseas cap under any circumstances and it would have needed a special ruling to bring them off. The service was read out of the little prayer book circulated by the Jewish Welfare Board, with which about a fourth of the congregation were already provided from the camps in the States. We read the abbreviated Hebrew service, then about half of the prayers in English, and had an English sermon. The only objection to these innovations came from the cantor, Corporal Cohen, a young man with a traditional Jewish background, who had gathered the other Jews in his company every Friday evening for a brief service and was generally looked up to (although not always followed) as a religious leader. My only way of convincing him was to inquire among some of the other men as to the number who did not understand Hebrew. When he saw that over half of the Jewish soldiers had no understanding of the Hebrew service he withdrew his insistent request for a strict traditionalism and I was saved the necessity of falling back on my military rank.

I was much amused after the several services at the number of young men who came to me, complaining about Cohen's rendering of the services and boasting of their own ability. I was able to give several of them the chance in the ensuing days and found out that it is easy to get a Hebrew reader, quite possible to find one who reads with feeling and understanding, but utterly impossible to pick up in the army a cantor with a trained voice.

Our arrangements were made under the approval of my commanding officer, the senior chaplain of the post, and few features of our service were more appreciated than the address of Chaplain Stull at our services on the second day of the festival. I had hesitated to invite him, and was therefore doubly surprised when he assured me that this was the third successive year that he had preached at a Jewish New Year service: two years before on the Mexican Border, the year before in training camp in the States and now in the American Forces in France, Chaplain Stull was a regular army chaplain of eighteen years standing, and his membership in the Methodist Episcopal church was less conspicuous in his makeup than his long experience in army life. His sermon was one of the outstanding events of our holy season. His explanation of the vital importance of the Service of Supply to the army at the front came with personal weight for he had just come back from the fighting forces to take a promotion in the rear. His moral interpretation of the significance of each man to the whole army was the sort of thing that the soldier needs and likes.

These services were unusual in that they were the first holy season which most of the men had spent away from home. The war was still on then; the St.

Mihiel drive took place the day after Rosh Hashana; the news from the front was usually good and always thrilling. We at the rear were deeply stirred. Some of us had been wounded and were now recovering; some were in training and were soon to leave for the front; some were in the S. O. S. permanently. But the shadow of war was dark upon us all. We were in the uncertainty, the danger, the horror of it. We felt a personal thrill at the words of the prayers,—"Who are to live and who to die; who by the sword and who by fire." We recited with personal fervor the memorial prayer for our fallen comrades. Many among us were eager to give thanks at recovery from wounds. Therefore, the desire for a religious observance of our solemn days was all the greater. Men came in from a hundred miles, often walking ten miles to a train before they could ride the rest.

Brothers, long separated, often met by chance, soon to separate again for an unknown future. I remember two—one a veteran of two battles, now convalescing at a hospital, the other newly arrived from the States and still in training. They met on Rosh Hashanah, each ignorant of the other's whereabouts and the veteran not even knowing whether his brother had arrived in France. The touching scene of their reunion had its humorous side too, for the wounded soldier from the hospital naturally had not a franc in his possession, and the boy from the States had enough money for a real holiday and had reserved a hotel room with a luxurious French bed. He was thus able to act as host for two happy days and nights. But on Yom Kippur when the wounded soldier came again his brother was not there. His unit had been ordered to the front and I do not know whether they ever met again.

War had us all in its iron grip. I, for one, expected soon to have my request granted that I be assigned to a combat division. Not that I overlooked the need for Jewish work in the S. O. S., but the most pressing need at that time was at the front, and I was looking forward to taking up the more exacting duties there.

The three Jewish families of the city added a pathetic touch, for they were glad indeed to attend a Jewish service and for the sake of the soldiers were willing to sit through our English additions. Their situation seemed similar to that of most recent immigrants of the United States; the parents spoke both Yiddish and French, the young people like ours in America, spoke chiefly the language of the country. It was both ludicrous and touching to see American soldiers competing to exchange the few French words they knew with the two or three Jewish daughters. It was often their first chance for a word with a girl of their own class, certainly with a Jewish girl, since they had left America. And the fact that the girl with her familiar appearance could not communicate with them on a conversational basis, did not seem to impede their relations in the least. The isolated condition of these French Jews in a city of 30,000 can only be compared to that of American Jews in a country village.

While at Nevers I could not overlook the opportunity to visit the two great hospital centers at Mars and at Mesves sur Loire. I visited from ward to ward in both of them, paying special attention to the Jewish boys and finding always plenty of occasion for favors of a hundred different kinds. At that time we were short of chaplains of all denominations in the army, so that even the hospitals had not enough to minister fully to their thousands of sick and wounded, while the convalescent camps with their hundreds of problems were almost uncared for in this respect.

At Mars I held a service on Friday night which was fairly typical of conditions in France. The service was announced as a Jewish religious service, but on my arrival I found the Red Cross room crowded with men of every type, including four negroes in the front row. Evidently it was the only place the men had outside the wards, so they came there every night for the show, movie, or service which might be provided. They were not merely respectful to the service and the minority of Jews who took part in it. They were actively responsive to the message I brought them of conditions in America and the backing the people at home were giving them in their great work abroad. These wounded men from the lines, these medical corpsmen who might never see the front, were alike eager to feel the part they personally were playing in the great, chaotic outlines of the world-wide struggle. And they responded to a Jewish service with an interest which I soon found was typical of the soldier, in his restless attention, his open-mindedness, his intolerance of cant but love of genuine religion.

The meetings and partings of war-time came home to me several times at Nevers. I was called to see a young man in the hospital, suffering from spinal meningitis. I found him a highly intelligent boy from Chicago who knew a number of my old friends there. I was able to do a few minor favors for him such as obtaining his belongings and notifying his unit that he was not absent without leave, but simply locked up in the contagious ward. But on his recovery the news went to his family in Chicago to get in touch with my wife and a friendship was established on a genuine basis of interests in common. At another time I was approached at the Y. M. C. A. by one of their women workers who had heard my name announced. She turned out to be a Mrs. Campbell of my old home town, Sioux City, Iowa, and an acquaintance of my mother through several charity boards of which they both were members. She was acting as instructor in French and adviser to the American soldiers in Nevers, while her husband, Prof. Campbell of Morningside College, was on the French front with the French auxiliary of the Y. M. C. A.

Another interesting incident was my meeting with Mr. Julius Rosenwald of Chicago, then touring France as a member of the National Council of Defense. The Y. M. C. A. secretary asked me to introduce him to a soldier audience in one of their huts. The first day I came, however, Mr. Rosenwald was delayed and the boys had to put up with a new film of Douglas Fairbanks in his stead, like good soldiers accepting the substitution gladly enough. On the second day Mr. Rosenwald himself was there and I had the pleasure of introducing him to an audience of about five hundred soldiers, as varied a group as ever wore the American uniform. His simple personal appeal was a direct attempt to build up the morale of the troops through a hearty report of the interest and enthusiasm of the people at home. He called for a show of hands of the home states of the different men, then responded by reading letters and telegrams from governors and other local officials.   Mr. Rosenwald was one of the very few official travelers in France whose trip was not merely informative to himself but also valuable to the army. We in the army grew to dislike "joy riders" so heartily that it is a positive pleasure to mention such a conspicuous exception.

Another duty typical of the variety of tasks which welcomed me as a chaplain, was to conduct the defense of a Jewish boy at a general court martial. He asked to see me during the holydays, told me his story, and I stayed over in Nevers a few days to act as his counsel. Since that time I have frequently been called on for advice in similar cases, for an army chaplain has almost as many legal and medical duties as strictly religious ones. In this particular case circumstantial evidence seemed to show that the young man had stolen and sold some musical instruments from an army warehouse where he worked. He was only a boy, a volunteer who had falsified his age in order to enlist. According to his own story he was partially involved in the case, acting ignorantly as agent for the real criminal.

The trial was quite fair, bringing out the circumstantial evidence against him, and his sentence was as low as could possibly be expected. So, with memories of friendships made, of work accomplished, of a new world opening ahead, I left Nevers on September

20th after only eighteen days of service. I had to report at Chaumont again to receive my orders to join the 27th Division.

For two months after that no Jewish chaplain was stationed in the Intermediate Section, which covered the entire central part of France and contained many thousands of American troops, including everywhere a certain proportion of Jews. Then Chaplain Rabinowitz reported at Nevers temporarily and served for his entire time in France in various points in the Intermediate Section, at Nevers, Blois and at St. Aignan.

I had been thrust into the midst of this tremendous, crying need for service of every kind, religious, personal and military. I went to my division to find the same or greater need, as the situation was always more tense at the actual front. For three weeks I had ministered as much as I could to the Jewish men scattered about Nevers and all through the central portion of France. Now I left them for good. Their usual greeting on meeting me had been, "You are the first Jewish chaplain or worker we have met on this side." And unfortunately, the same greeting was addressed to me every time I came to a new unit or city until the very day I left France. The need among these two million soldiers was so tremendous that a hundred times our resources would not have been sufficient. As it was, we made no pretense at covering the field, but simply did day labor wherever we were stationed, serving the soldiers, Jews and Christians alike, and giving our special attention to the religious services and other needs of the Jewish men.

CHAPTER III

I REACHED my division on the first of October, 1918, after a tedious ten days on the way. I traveled most of the way with Lieutenant Colonel True, whom I met on the train coming out of Chaumont. I found that the higher ranking officers invariably approached the chaplains not as officers of inferior rank but as leaders of a different kind, much as a prominent business man treats his minister in civil life. Colonel True was a regular army man of long standing who was being transferred from another division to the Twenty-Seventh. When we arrived at the Hotel Richmond, the Y. M. C. A. hotel for officers in Paris, we found only one room available with a double bed, and so for the first time in my life I had the honor of sleeping with a Lieutenant Colonel. The honor was a doubtful one as he had at the time a slight attack of "flu" brought on from exposure and a touch of gas in the recent St. Mihiel drive. Colonel True had received his promotion from a majority and his transfer before the drive, but had not reported until he had gone through the whole fight at the head of his battalion. I mention this not as a striking, but strictly as a typical proceeding on the part of the average American officer.

For a few days we were held at the Replacement

Camp at Eu in Normandy—an idyllic spot within sight of the English Channel, surrounded by gentle hills. While there I made several trips to Tréport, a favorite summer resort on the Channel before the war. It is a quaint little fishing village with a typical modern summer resort superimposed. The old stone Norman cottages with their high roofs always had a touch of decoration somewhere, in mosaic, paint or stained glass, different from the plainer architecture of Central France. The modern part consists of several beautiful hotels and a number of cheap restaurants and curio shops. Of course, the hotels were all used by the British Army as hospitals at this time. I visited Base Hospital 16, a Philadelphia Unit, which was loaned to the British. I had a delightful talk with our Red Cross Chaplain and made a tour of many of the wards. The patients were almost all British with a few Americans from the August campaign in Flanders. Among the rest I met about a dozen Jewish boys, English and Australian, who were naturally delighted by the rare visit of a Jewish Chaplain. The eight Jewish Chaplains in the British Expeditionary Forces were attached to the various Army Headquarters, and so had to cover impossible areas in their work. The nearest one to Tréport was Rabbi Geffen at Boulogne with whom I afterward came into communication, and from whom I obtained a large number of the army prayer books arranged by the Chief Rabbi of England for use in the British Forces.

Hospital visiting is dreary work, especially when there is action going on from which one is separated. The work is exhausting physically, walking up and down the long wards and stopping by bedsides. It is especially a drain on the nerves and sympathies, to see so many sick and mutilated boys—boys in age most of them, certainly boys in spirit—and giving oneself as the need arises. And in a hospital so many men have requests. They are helpless and it is always impossible to have enough visitors and enough chaplains for them. I was glad to be useful at Tréport but gladder still when the word came through to release all troops in the Second Corps Replacement Depot.

We were loaded on a train, the soldiers in box-cars of the familiar type("40 men or 8 horses") with the little group of officers crowded together in a single first-class coach. Broken windows, flat wheels and no lights showing—we were beginning to feel that we were in the war zone. From Eu to Peronne took from 4:30 A. M. to 9:30 P. M. with three changes of trains and ten additional stops. We got only a short view of the railroad station at Amiens, at that time almost completely destroyed. Our division was then in the British area on the Somme sector, and at the time of our arrival they had just come out of the great victory at the Hindenburg Line.

Our first ruined city was Peronne, which will never leave my memory. The feeling of a ruined town is absolutely indescribable, for how can one imagine a town with neither houses nor people, where the very streets have often been destroyed? This situation contradicts our very definition of a town, for a town is made of streets, houses and people; no imagination can quite grasp the reality of war and ruin without its actual experience. And Peronne was much more striking than most cities in the war zone; it had been fought through six different times, and its originally stately public buildings showed only enough to impress us with the ruin that had been wrought. Only one wall of one end of the church was standing, with two fine Gothic arches, only one side of the building on the square and so on through the whole town. We became inured to the sight of ruined villages later on, but the first shock of seeing Peronne will be indelible.

The headquarters of the division were then located at the Bois de Buire, about ten miles out, though for almost a half day we could find nobody to give us exact directions. At last Lieutenant Colonel H. S. Sternberger, the division quartermaster, put in an appearance and offered to take me and Lieutenant Colonel True up to headquarters in his car. The rest of our party had all wandered off by then in the direction of their various units. Colonel Sternberger was the highest ranking officer at the time among the thousand Jews in the Twenty-Seventh Division. Lieutenant Colonel Morris Liebman of the 106th Infantry, also a Jew, had been killed in action in Flanders six weeks before, a loss which was very deeply felt in his regiment. Colonel Sternberger was one of the popular staff officers of the division owing to his indefatigable labors for the welfare of the boys. His great efforts at the expense of much personal risk and of serious damage to his health were directed to get the food up to the front on time. While I was with the division, Colonel Sternberger proved both a staunch personal friend and an active ally in my work.

It took more than a day to become acquainted with the camouflaged offices in the woods. Small huts, with semicircular iron roofs covered with branches, were scattered about among the trees. Some of them had signs, Division Adjutant, Commanding General, and the rest; others were billets. I invariably lost my way when I went to lunch and wandered for some minutes before finding "home." "Home" was a hut exactly like the rest, where the French mission and the gas officer had their offices during the day and where six of us slept at night. I fell heir to the cot of one of the interpreters then home on leave, Georges Lévy, who afterward became one of my best friends. My baggage had disappeared on the trip, so that I had only my hand bag with the little it could hold. My first need, naturally, was for blankets to cover the cot. I collected these from various places, official and otherwise, until the end of the month found me plentifully provided. I must admit that the first cool nights in the woods forced me to sleep in my clothes. Naturally, my first task was to wire for my baggage, but it had completely vanished and did not return for four long months. Everybody lost his possessions at some time during the war; I was unique only in losing them at the outset and not seeing them until the whole need for them was over.

The boys had just come out of the line, worn out, with terrible losses, but after a great victory such as occurs only a few times in any war. They had broken the Hindenburg Line, that triple row of trenches and barbed wire, with its concrete pill-boxes, its enfilading fire from machine guns, its intricate and tremendous system of defenses. I crossed the line many times during the month that followed and never failed to marvel that human beings could ever have forced it. The famous tunnel of the St. Quentin Canal was in our sector, too, as well as part of the canal itself. The villages about us were destroyed so completely that no single roof or complete wall was standing for a shelter and the men had to live in the cellars.

One wall always bore the name of the former village in large letters, which became still larger and more striking in the territory near the Hindenburg Line, so long occupied by the Germans. I used to repay the generous Tommies for their rides on the constant stream of trucks (we called them "lorries," like the English) by translating the numerous German signs at railroad crossings and the like, about which they always had much curiosity.

One could travel anywhere on main roads by waiting until a truck came along and then hailing it. If the seat was occupied there was usually some room in the rear, and the British drivers were always glad to take one on and equally glad to air their views on the war. When one came to a cross road, he jumped off, hailed the M. P. (Military Police) for directions and took the next truck which was going in the proper direction. In that way I have often traveled on a dozen trucks in a day, with stop-overs and occasional walks of a few miles to fill in the gaps. Between a map, a compass and the M. P.'s, we always managed to circulate and eventually find our way home again.

We saw the heavy guns lumbering on their way to the front, the aëroplanes humming overhead like a swarm of dragon-flies. Day and night we could hear the rumble of guns like distant thunder, while at night the flashes showed low on the horizon like

heat lightning. Our salvage depot was at Tincourt
at the foot of the hill, and when I went over there
Corporal Klein and Sergeant Friedlander were
quick to repair gaps in my equipment. One night
I witnessed the division musical comedy (the
"Broadway Boys") in an old barn at Templeux
le Fosse, where we walked in the dark, found the
place up an alley and witnessed a really excellent
performance with costumes, scenery and real or-
chestra. In the middle of an act, an announcement
would be made that all men of the third battalion,
108th Infantry, should report back at once, and a
group of fellows would rise and file out for the five-
mile hike back in the darkness: they were to move up
to the front before morning.

My chief effort during those few hurried days
was to get into touch with the various units so that
I could be of some definite service to them when they
went into action. Unfortunately, almost every time
I arranged for a service and appeared to hold it the
"outfit" would already be on the move. The best
service I held was at the village of Buire, where
about forty boys gathered together under the trees
among the ruined houses. They were a deeply devotional group, told me about their holyday services
conducted by a British army chaplain at Doulens,
about their fallen comrades for whom they wanted to
repeat the memorial prayers, and about their own
narrow escapes for which they were eager to offer
thanks. They had the deep spiritual consciousness
which comes to most men in moments of great peril.

I managed to reach most of the infantry regiments,
however, by hiking down from the woods and sometimes catching a ride. Everywhere was action. It

was the breathing space between our two great battles of the war. Every unit was hoping and expecting a long rest. But that hope could not be fulfilled. The intensity of the drive against the entire German line was beginning to tell and every possible unit was needed in the line to push ahead. So the rest of the Twenty-Seventh Division was brief indeed. Every regiment was starting for the front with no replacements after the terrific slaughter of two weeks before, with very little new equipment and practically no rest. And the front was now further away than it had been. The success of the allied forces meant longer marches for our tired troops.

All the villages were devasted in this area. It was the section between Peronne and the old Hindenburg Line. Not until we came to the German side of the Hindenburg Line did we find the villages in any sort of repair. The men lived in cellars without roofs, in rooms without walls or sometimes in barracks which were constructed by either of the opposing armies during the long years of the struggle. Of course, many shelters existed such as our "elephant huts" in the woods or the perfect honeycomb of dugouts in the sides of the quarry at Templeux le Gerard.

One day I "lorried" up to the division cemeteries near the old battlefield, which were being laid out by a group of chaplains with a large detail of enlisted men. I saw the occasional Jewish graves marked with the Star of David and later was able to complete the list and have all Jewish graves in our division similarly marked. I got to know the country about Bellicourt and Bony, where our heaviest fighting had taken place. I heard the story of the eight British tanks, lying helpless at the top of the long ridge near Bony, where they had run upon a mine field. I got to know the "Ausies," always the best friends and great admiration of our soldiers, with their dashing courage and reckless heroism, and the "Tommies," those steady, matter-of-fact workmen at the business of war, whom our boys could never quite understand.

Finally our headquarters moved forward, too. I jumped out of a colonel's car one dark night and hunted for an hour and a half among the hills before I found the chalk quarry where they now were hidden from prying air scouts. At last, finding the quarry, I met a boy I knew, who took me to the dugout where the senior chaplain was sleeping. I crawled into a vacant bunk, made myself at home and left the next morning for good. The quarry did not appeal to me when wet; one was too likely to slide from the top to the bottom and stay there; and I had no desire to test its advantages when dry. The next time I came back to headquarters they were in the village of Joncourt, beyond the Hindenburg Line, in territory which we had released from the Germans. The chief attraction of Joncourt was an occasional roof —of course, there were no windows. The cemetery had been used as a "strong point" by the retreating Germans, who had scattered the bodies about and used the little vaults as pill-boxes in which to mount machine guns. And our message center was located in a German dugout fully fifty feet underground; evidently plenty of precautions had been taken against allied air raids. In fact, from this point on every house in every village had a conspicious sign, telling of the *Fliegerschutz* for a certain number of men in its cellar. In addition, the placard told the number of officers, men and horses which could be accommodated with billets on the premises. Evidently, the Germans in laying out their permanently occupied territory, went about it in their usual business-like fashion.

But between my glimpses of these various headquarters, I was at the front with the troops going into the trenches and had had a glimpse of war. My first experience under fire was in some woods near Maretz, where I spent part of the night with one battalion, as they paused before going into the trenches. I finished the night on the floor of a house in the village, having grown accustomed enough to the sound of the shells to sleep in spite of it. Like most people I had wondered how one feels under fire, and experienced a queer sensation when I first heard the long whine of a distant shell culminating in a sudden explosion. Now I realized that I was under fire, too. But I speedily found that one feels more curiosity than fear under long-distance fire; real fear comes chiefly when the shells begin to land really near by. I was to experience that, too, a little later. In fact, I found out soon that every soldier is frightened; a good soldier is simply one who does his duty in spite of fear.

Then a report came in that Chaplain John Ward, of the 108th Infantry, had been seriously wounded and I was sent to take his place with the unit. In a push the chaplain works with the wounded; after it, with the dead. Of many sad duties at the front, his is perhaps the saddest of all. My first station was with the third battalion headquarters and aid

post in a big white house set back in a little park
in the tiny village of Escaufourt, a mile or so behind the lines. Captain Merrill was in command
of the battalion and one could see how the work and
responsibility wore on him day by day, reducing the
round, cheerful soldier for the time almost to a
whispering, tottering old man. But his spirit held
him to the task; he slept for only a few minutes at a
time, and then was back at work again. A con-
scientious man can have no more exacting duty than
this, to care for the lives of a thousand men.

We were under constant fire there, though not
under observation, but the little ambulances ran up
to the gate of the château for the wounded, who had
to walk or be carried in and out from the house to the
gate. We ate upstairs in the stately dining room
at times, though we usually ate and always slept
in the crowded cellar where the major and his staff
were housed. There eight or nine of us would sit on
our brick seats and sleep with our backs against the
wall, being awakened from time to time by a messenger coming in or by the ringing of the field telephone in the corner. The telephone operator was
always testing one or another connection, day
and night, for the emergency when it would be
needed.

One night companies H and I of the 108th Infantry
were almost completely wiped out by gas. They
were in low lying trenches by the side of the canal
under a constant fire of gas shells, while the damp
weather kept the dangerous fumes near the ground.
They had no orders to evacuate to a safer post and
no human being can live forever in a gas mask, so
one after another the men yielded to temptation, took

off their masks for momentary relief, and inhaled the gas-laden air. All evening and night they kept coming in by twos and threes to our aid post, the stronger ones walking, the rest on stretchers. Their clothing reeked of the sickeningly sweet odor. The room was soon full of it, so that we had to blow out the candles and open the door for a few minutes to avoid being gassed ourselves. There were three ambulances running that night to the Main Dressing Station, and I made it my task to meet each car, notify the doctor and bring the gassed and wounded men out to the ambulance. Most of them were blinded for the time being by the effect of the gas. No light was possible, as that would have drawn fire at once. Every ten minutes through the night our village was shelled, and in walking the forty or fifty yards through the park to the gate, I had to make two detours with my blinded men to avoid fresh shell-holes made that very afternoon. I admit feeling an occasional touch of panic as I led the big helpless fellows around those fresh shell holes and helped them into the ambulances. The final touch came when a youngster of perhaps seventeen entered the aid post alone, walking painfully. "What outfit are you from, sonny?" was my natural greeting. "I am the last man left in Company H," was the proud reply.

This was the sort of fatal blunder which seemed to occur once in every command before the lesson was learned that gas-filled trenches need no defending, and that troops, safely withdrawn a hundred yards or more, can be moved forward again quickly enough the moment the gas lifts. The English had had the same lesson more than once until they learned it thoroughly; so had the Germans; now our armies, with their examples before us, had to learn it again through the suffering of our own soldiers. Our division was not the only one in which the same or a similar blunder cost the men so dearly, for I have read the same incident of more than one unit on other parts of the American line, and have had them verified by officers who were present at those other catastrophes. In the art of war the instruction of the generals costs the lives of the soldiers.

We had the peculiar experience of seeing the village which we had entered in good condition crumbling about us under the enemy fire. Even the windows were intact when we reached it; the Germans were just out, and our artillery had been outstripped completely in the forward rush. Under the constant pounding of back area fire, designed to prevent ammunition and supplies coming up to the line unmolested, our little village lost windows, roofs and walls, disintegrating steadily into a heap of ruins.

One evening we were assigned the task of evacuating some old French peasants who had clung to their little homes through all the world-shaking catastrophe. At last they had to leave, as the danger to them was too direct and, in addition, they constituted a hidden menace to our troops in case even one of them had been left behind as a spy. I went with a party of Australians and a few of our men to the houses in the outskirts of the town, where the greatest danger existed. I remember the utterly disconsolate attitude of two old men and a little old woman in one of them, when they were told they had to leave. They seemed numb in the midst

of all the rush and roar of warfare. Their little possessions were there, they were of the peasant type
and had probably never been out of the district in
their lives. The advance of the enemy in 1914 had
been accompanied by no fighting near their homes,
and now the allied victory, the one hope of their
country, was the one thing that bore destruction to
their little village and tore them away from the spot
where they were rooted.

One evening I joined a ration party going forward and visited the lines and advanced headquarters at St. Souplet, hearing the peculiar whistle
of a sniper's bullet pass me as I made my way back
after dusk. One of the boys carrying a heavy bag
of hardtack had a sore shoulder, not quite well
from a previous wound. So I shouldered his bag
for a decidedly weary mile of skulking along a
sunken road and hurrying across the occasional
open spaces. When we came to his unit I was
glad to turn the bag over to him; I felt no pleasure
in such lumpy burden, and would far rather have
worn out my shoulder with something more appreciated by the boys than hardtack,—the one thing
which nobody enjoyed but which was eaten only
because they were desperately hungry. On the night
of October 16th we all moved over, preparatory to
the push across the Selle River. We installed ourselves in the large building at the cross roads, where
the aid post was stationed. I joined a group of
sleepers on the cellar floor, picking my way in the
darkness to find a vacant spot. My trench coat on
the plank floor made a really luxurious bed.

The next morning, October 17th, I was awakened
at 5:20 by the barrage; the boys were going over;

the battle of the Selle River had begun. By six o'clock the wounded began to flow in, at first by twos and threes, then in a steady stream. They came walking wearily along or were carried on the shoulders of German prisoners or occasionally by our own men. As we were at the crossroads, we got most of the wounded, English, German and American, as well as a great deal of the shelling with which back areas are always deluged during an attack. In this case, our post was just behind the lines at first, but it became a back area within a very few days owing to the dash and brilliancy of our tired troops when the orders came to go over the top. They stormed the heights across the stream after wading it in the first rush, and then went on across the hills and fields.

Our attack was a part of the campaign of the British Third Army and a small element in the great "push" going on at that time over the entire front. Our task with that of the Thirtieth Division on our right was to cross the Selle River and advance toward the Sambre Canal. On our left were British troops, while we were supported by Australian artillery and the British Air Service. In our first great battle, that of the Hindenburg Line, the "Ausies" had acted as the second wave, coming up just in time to save some of the hard pressed units of our Division and to complete the success of our assault. So we knew them well enough and were glad indeed to have their excellent artillery to put over the barrage for our second attack.

The Australians and, in fact, all the British Colonial troops, had much more in common with the American soldiers than had the British troops themselves. They were like our men, young, hardy, dashing. They were all volunteers. They had a type of discipline of their own, which included saluting their own officers when they wanted to and never saluting British officers under any circumstances. I took a natural pride in hearing of their commanding officer, Lieutenant General Sir John Monash, who held the highest rank of any Jew in the war. It was no little honor to be the commander of those magnificent troops from Australia.

Meanwhile we were busy at the first aid post. I found myself the only person at hand who could speak any German, so I took charge of the door, with a group of prisoners to carry the wounded in and out and load them in the ambulances. As soon as my dozen or so prisoners were tired out I would send them on to the "cage" and pick up new men from the constant stream flowing in from the front. Our opponents here were chiefly Wurtembergers, young boys of about twenty, although one regiment of Prussian marines was among them. Among the first prisoners were two German physicians who offered to assist ours in the work. They worked all day, one in our aid post, the other in that of the 107th Infantry, side by side with our surgeons and doing excellent work for Americans and Germans alike. They picked their own assistants from among their captured medical corpsmen, and were strictly professional in their attitude throughout. One of them was Dr. Beckhard, a Jew from Stuttgart, with whom I had a few snatches of conversation and whom I should certainly like to meet again under more congenial circumstances. I was amused in the midst of it all when the doctor noticed his brother, an ar-

tilleryman, coming in as one of the endless file of
stretcher bearers, carrying wounded in gray or olive
drab. The doctor asked me whether he might take
his brother as one of his assistants for the day.
"Is he any good?" I asked. "Oh, yes," was the
answer, "as good as any medical orderly." So I
gave permission and the two, together with a real
medical orderly and another young prisoner as interpreter, ran one room of the first aid post in their
own way. I kept an American soldier on guard there
chiefly to be prepared for any eventualities; as a
matter of fact the German surgeons treated American wounded and American surgeons treated German wounded with the same impartial spirit. The
two physicians joined the other prisoners at the
end of the day bearing letters of appreciation written
by Captain Miller, the surgeon in charge of our
post.

About a year later when communication with Germany was opened again, I found that this chance
meeting at the front proved an odd means of communication with my German cousins. When Dr.
Beckhard returned to Stuttgart he lectured on his
experiences at the front, mentioning among other
things that he had met an American Rabbi by the
name of Levinger. Some distant relatives of mine
living in the city heard the talk and wrote to a
nearer branch of the family living in another part
of Wurtemberg, so that shortly after the actual experience they knew of my being in the army and
serving at the front.

Only the small Ford ambulances could come as
near the front as our post, while the larger ones
came only to the Advanced Dressing Station at

Busigny. These smaller ambulances were unable to accommodate the constant stream of gassed and wounded men coming from the lines. Those who had minor wounds, especially in the arms, had to be directed along the proper road according to that ironical term, "walking wounded." Cases which in civil life would be carried to an ambulance, given full treatment, and then driven gently to the nearest hospital, were here given emergency dressings and told, "The Advanced Dressing Station is two miles down that road, boys. Walk slow and don't miss the sign telling where to turn to the left." Other more serious cases for whom there was no room in ambulances, at the moment were carried on stretchers by prisoners. I would assemble three or four such cases, take a revolver left by some wounded officer or non-com, and give it to a "walking wounded" with instructions to "see that they get safely to the next point." Naturally, these boys with minor wounds of their own were safe guardians to see that the German prisoners did their duty. I can still see their grins as they assured me: "Those fellows are sure going to stick on the job, sir. I'll say they will!" The attitude of the slightly wounded men was often full of grim humor. I remember one Australian carried in on a stretcher who called me to his side with their customary "Here, Yank," and when I responded handed me very gravely a Mills bomb which he had used to overawe his captive bearers, apparently threatening to blow them up with himself should they prove insubordinate.

A constant worry of mine were the weapons which the wounded men dropped in front or within the

aid post. Knowing that all army supplies would
be reissued to them on release from the hospital, the
soldiers did not care to carry heavy rifles or even re-
volvers and bombs back with them. The result was
a pile of weapons at just the point where my
prisoner stretcher-bearers could have easy access
to them. I kept an M. P. busy much of the time
removing these to a place of comparative safety.

Behind the aid post we found a shed which served
as temporary morgue for the men who died before
we could give them emergency treatment and rush
them off in the ambulances. The extreme tension
of the actual fight and the tremendous pressure of
administering to the living calloused the heart
for the moment to these horrible necessities, which
come back to memory in later days with the full
measure of ghastly detail.

The chaplain is the handy man at the front, one
of the few who is not limited by special duties or
confined to a particular spot. He works forward or
backward as the need exists. He ladles out hot
chocolate with the Red Cross, carries a stretcher
with the Medical Corps, ties up a bandage when that
is needed, and prays for Jew and Christian alike.
I ministered to a number of Jewish and Christian
soldiers who were dying, leading the Jews in the
traditional confession of faith, and reading a psalm
for the Protestants. One of the surgeons came to
me and said, "Captain Connor here is dying, and
Chaplain Hoffman our priest is at Battalion Headquarters acting as interpreter to examine some
prisoners. What can we do?" So I borrowed the
surgeon's rosary and held the cross to the lips of
the dying Catholic. This incident, so impossible

in civil life, is really expected among soldiers,—it has been repeated so many times and in so many different ways.

We were constantly under heavy shell fire, as our place at the cross roads was not only convenient of access, but was also the only route for bringing supplies and ammunition to our part of the front. Once as I was in the middle of the road with several prisoners loading stretchers on an ambulance, a shell burst in a pool about twenty feet away, covering us with a shower of mud. My prisoners, who had a wholesome respect for their own artillery, could hardly be prevented from dropping the stretcher. However, we were too near the explosion to be hurt, as the fragments flew over our heads, killing one boy and wounding four others across the street. One of the wounded was an American runner from the front, who was enjoying a hasty bite at the army field kitchen around the corner. He came over in a hurry to have his cheek tied up and then went calmly back to the field kitchen to finish his interrupted lunch. The man who was killed was standing about seventy-five feet from the spot of the explosion beside the motor-cycle which he drove, waiting for his commanding officer to come and use the side-car. He pitched forward as though falling to avoid the explosion, just as we would have done if we had not been holding a stretcher. When he did not rise, Father Kelley and I went over to him and found that a fatal bit of metal had struck him in the head just below his steel helmet.

And so the work went on. The next day we heard of some wounded who had not yet been brought in from Bandival Farm. Chaplain Burgh of the 107th

Infantry and I gathered together a few volunteers of our ambulance men and several prisoners to go out and carry them in. It was about a mile and a half out across the battlefield under intermittent shell fire. I placed my captured Luger revolver, which one of the boys had brought me the day before, in a conspicuous position with the handle projecting from my front pocket. I had had the thing unloaded as soon as I got it because I preferred not to run any unnecessary risks. Being a non-combatant both by orders and inclination, I was afraid it might go off. But my prisoners did not know that and so I had no difficulty in silencing their muttered protests against such a hard and dangerous hike. Working prisoners under fire like this was strictly against international law, but that sort of a provision we violated frankly and cheerfully. On the way back with our wounded across the muddy and shell-pitted fields, we passed German machine gun emplacements with the dead gunners still beside the guns, Americans lying with their faces toward the enemy, and constant heaps of supplies of all kinds strewn about. One of our stretchers was put down for a moment's rest near such a scattered group of German knapsacks. One of the prisoners asked if he might help himself, and when I nodded all four made a wild dash for the supplies and each man came back carrying an army overcoat and a bag of emergency rations, the little sweetish crackers which they carried instead of our hard tack.

On the third day of the attack I joined two men of the Intelligence Department in walking out to the front line, then over five miles from the village. It was a hard hike through the mud and about the

shell holes. Finally we found our friends dug in
(for the fourth time that day) on a little ridge.
Each time their temporary trenches had been completed orders had come either for a short retreat
or a further advance, and now by the middle of the
afternoon the boys were digging another at the
place where they were to stay till the next morning. Across the ravine in a little wood the Germans
were hanging on for the time being until their artillery could be saved. I visited the 108th Infantry
in reserve and emptied my musette bag of the sacks
of Bull Durham which I had brought along from
the Red Cross. Then the boys wanted matches,
which I had forgotten, and their gratitude was lost
in their disgust.

I found Captain Merrill with his staff inspecting
two captured German 77's, on which they had just
placed the name of their unit. By that time, after
three consecutive battles without replacements, our
units were so depleted that a regiment had only 250
rifles in the line instead of the original 3,000. Captain Merrill's battalion consisted on that day of
87 riflemen. Just as we finished our inspection of
the guns the enemy artillery started "strafing"
again, so we jumped into a shell-hole which had
been hollowed out into convenient form and finished
our conversation there. I then visited some of the
107th Infantry in the front line rifle pits, one hundred yards or so ahead, and turned back again
toward the village.

I was just losing my way among the hills with
approaching twilight, when I met an Australian artillery train on their way back for supplies, and
climbed on a limber to ride into town. It was a wild

ride, with the rough roads and the drivers' habit of trotting over the spots where shell-holes showed that danger might linger. I held on in quite unmilitary fashion and wondered if the horse behind would be careful when I fell. But they brought me in safely and added one more means of locomotion to the dozens which I had utilized at various times: ammunition "lorries," ambulances, side-cars and even a railway locomotive—everything in fact except a tank.

The next day we breathed more freely again. Our tired boys, reduced in numbers, weakened in physical resistance, but going forward day after day as their orders came, were at last to go out of the lines. Their job was done; they had reached the Sambre Canal; and though we did not know it, they were not to go into battle again. I lorried back to Joncourt, the temporary division headquarters, for the night, changed my clothes, slept in a borrowed cot, read a very heartening pile of home letters which had accumulated for some weeks, and returned to St. Souplet the next day for the burial detail. It was the 21st of October; while the division as a whole marched back to the railhead, five chaplains with a detail of a hundred and fifty men stayed behind for the sad work that remained to be done.

At this time I stopped off at the 108th Infantry for a few minutes, as they halted for a meal after coming out of the lines, and had my orderly, David Lefkowitz, detached from his unit to serve with me for my entire remaining period with the division. I had become acquainted with him during my first few days in the division and found that he would be interested to work with me as orderly and assistant. The order assigning him to this special work was made out before we left the woods at Buire. But our various units were so depleted at the time that I arranged to leave him with his "outfit" for the battle. It was a serious deprivation to me, as Lefkowitz had been through the earlier battle at the Hindenburg Line and could have given me much assistance and advice in the front line work. Now that the fighting was over, he left his company to go with me and enjoy the comparative luxury of division headquarters until he rejoined his company to sail home from France. He was one of the many Jewish soldiers who welcomed the presence of a chaplain and gladly coöperated in every possible way to make my work successful.

Chaplain Francis A. Kelley, in charge of our burial work, laid out the cemetery on a hill overlooking the village and the battlefield. The rest of us searched the field with details of men, brought in the bodies on limbers, searched and identified them as well as possible. In doubtful cases the final identification was made at the cemetery, where men from every regiment were working and where most soldiers would have some one to recognize them. In addition, we buried German dead on the field, marking the graves and keeping a record of their location for the Graves Registration Service. A hundred and fifty-two men were buried there at St. Souplet, the last cemetery of the Twenty-Seventh Division in their battle grounds of France. The last body of all, found after the work had been finished and the men released from duty, was buried by us chaplains and the surgeon, who went out under the leadership of Father Kelley and dug the grave ourselves. Every evening the six of us gathered about our grate fire and relaxed from the grim business of the day. If we had allowed ourselves to dwell on it, we would have been incapable of carrying on the work: it was so ghastly, so full of pathetic and horrible details. We sang, played checkers, argued on religion. Imagine us singing the "Darktown Strutters' Ball," or discussing the fundamental principles of Judaism and Christianity for several hours! The five of us were all of different creeds, too—Catholic, Baptist, Christian, Christian Scientist and Jew. Our coöperation and our congeniality were typical of the spirit of the service throughout.

On the last day we held our burial service. We gathered together at the cemetery with a large flag spread out in the middle of the plot. I read a brief Jewish service, followed by Chaplains Bagby and Stewart in the Protestant and Father Kelley in the Catholic burial service, and at the end the bugle sounded "taps" for all those men of different faiths lying there together. We could see and hear the shells bursting beyond the hill, probably a hostile scout had caught sight of us at work. Above floated a British aëroplane. Some English soldiers working on their burial plot nearby stopped their digging and listened to our service.

And so we said farewell to our lost comrades and to the war at the same time.

CHAPTER IV

AFTER THE ARMISTICE

AFTER the burial work at St. Souplet was over, great covered lorries took us back the sixty miles or more to Corbie, in the vicinity of Amiens, which was to be our rest area. We greeted its paved streets, its fairly intact houses, its few tiny shops, as the height of luxury. Here and there a roof was destroyed or a wall down, for the enemy had come within three miles of Corbie in their drives earlier in the year. But we were in rest and comparative plenty at last. We saw real civilians again, not merely the few old people and little children left behind in the towns we had liberated. We had regular meals again and a chance to purchase a few luxuries beside, such as French bread at a shop and hard candy at the "Y." We no longer heard the whine of the shell or whistle of the bullet, nor smelled gas, nor slept in cellars. I was even lucky enough to capture a thick spring mattress which, with my blankets, made a bed that even a certain staff colonel envied me. A home-made grate in the fire-place fitted it for a tiny coal fire; the window frames were re-covered with oiled paper; we read the London Daily Mail in its Paris edition only one day late, instead of seeing it every ten days and then often two weeks out of date.

My billet, which I obtained from the British town

major, was a tall, narrow house just off the principal square, very pleasant indeed in dry weather. Its chief defect was a huge shell-hole in the roof through which the water poured in torrents when it rained, so that we had to cover ourselves with our rubber shelter-halves when we slept at night. The shell-hole, however, was a constant source of fuel, and we burned the laths and wood-work, of which small pieces were lying all about the top floor, until we found means to obtain a small but steady supply of coal. The house afforded room, after I had preëmpted it, for the Senior Chaplain of the Division, the Division Burial Officer and myself, together with our three orderlies.

Even in dry weather there was some excitement about the old house. There was the time when some tipsy soldiers, seeing the light in the Senior Chaplain's room late at night, mistook the place for a café and came stumbling in for a drink. When they saw the chaplain, they suddenly sobered and accepted very gravely the drink of water he offered them from his canteen. On another day the old woman who owned the house came in with her son, a French lieutenant, to take away her furniture. We did not mind losing the pretty inlaid table— we were soldiers and could stand that—but our mattresses and chairs were a different matter. None of us could argue with her torrential flow of French, but Lieutenant Curtiss, the Burial Officer, suddenly felt his real attack of flu redoubled in violence and had to take to his mattress. So the old lady finally relented sufficiently to leave us our beds and a chair or two, while her son became our devoted friend at the price of an American cigar.

I think that I shall never forget Corbie, with its narrow streets, its half-ruined houses, its great ancient church of gray, with one transept a heap of ruins, and the straight rows of poplars on both sides of the Somme Canal,—a bit of Corot in the mist of twilight. I remember the quiet, gray square one day with the American band playing a medley from the "Chocolate Soldier," for all the world like a phonograph at home. I remember the great memorial review of the division by General O'Ryan in honor of our men who had fallen; the staff stood behind the General at the top of a long, gentle slope, with three villages in the distance, the church looming up with its square, ruined tower, and the men spread out before us, a vanishing mass of olive drab against the dull shades of early winter.

I remember the day when three of us chaplains made the long trip back to our division cemeteries at St. Emelie, Bony and Guillemont Farm to read the burial service over those many graves, the result of the terrible battle at the Hindenburg Line. Chaplain Burgh, Protestant, of the 105th Infantry, Chaplain Eilers, Catholic, of the 106th Infantry, and I were sent back the fifty miles or more by automobile for this duty. It happened that it rained that day, as on most days, and the car was an open one. So the few soldiers still about in that deserted region had the rare sight of three cold and dripping chaplains standing out in the mud and rain to read the burial services, one holding his steel helmet as an umbrella over the prayerbook from which the other read, and then accepting the same service in return. There was none of the panoply of war, no bugle, firing party or parade, just the prayer uttered for each man in the faith to which he was born or to which he had clung. We did not even know the religion of every man buried there, but we knew that our prayers would serve for all.

We were lucky to be in Corbie on November 11th when the armistice was signed. Day after day we had stopped at Division Headquarters to inspect the maps and study the color pins which were constantly moving forward across France and Belgium. It was a study that made us all drunk with enthusiasm. We were under orders to move toward the front again on the 9th of November and to enter the lines once more on November 14th. The men had had very little rest and no fresh troops had come up to fill the losses made by wounds, exposure and disease. Our men could never hold a full divisional area now; only the knowledge of the wonders they had already accomplished made us consider it possible that they could fight again so soon. Time after time when their strength and spirit seemed both exhausted they had responded and gone ahead. Now they deserved their rest.

We greeted the good news very calmly; the German prisoners were a little more elated; the French went mad with ecstasy. It was the only time I have ever seen Frenchmen drunk, heard them go home after midnight singing patriotic songs out of key. In Amiens, where several thousand of the inhabitants had returned by that time, the few restaurants were crowded and gaiety was unrestrained. I heard a middle-aged British lieutenant sing the "Marseillaise" with a pretty waitress in the "Café de la Cathédral" the following evening, and respond when asked to repeat it in the main dining room. He returned to our side room decidedly redder than he had gone out. "Why, the whole British general staff's in there!" he gasped. But he received only applause without a reprimand. The war was over and for the moment all France was overcome with joy and all the allied armies with relief and satisfaction.

After the armistice the front line work, with its absorption on the problems of the wounded and the dead, became a thing of the past. The chaplain could now turn to the more normal aspects of his work, to religious ministration, personal service, advice and assistance in the thousands of cases which came before him constantly. In fact, on the whole his work became much the same as it had been in training camp in the States. A few differences persisted; in France the chaplain was without the magnificent backing of the Jewish communities at home, which were always so eager to assist in entertaining and helping the Jewish men in the nearby camps. The Jewish Welfare Board with its excellent workers could never cover the entire field as well as it could at home in America. Then there were special problems because the men were so far away from home, because the mail service was poor, because worries about allotments were more acute than if home had been nearer, and because the alien civilization and language never made the men feel quite comfortable.

In the Corbie area the 27th Division was scattered about in twelve villages, the farthest one eight miles from division headquarters. Transportation was still common on the roads, though often I had to walk and once I made the trip to Amiens in the cab of a locomotive when neither train nor truck was running, and found a ride back in an empty ambulance which had brought patients to the evacuation hospital. The villages were almost deserted, and were in rather bad condition after their nearness to the German advance of 1918, so that the men could be crowded together and were very easy to reach in a body. I began making regular visits to the various units of the division, meeting the men, holding services, receiving their requests and carrying them out as well as possible. And I was constantly making new acquaintances, as the wounded and sick began coming back from the hospitals to rejoin the division.

I had the opportunity of an occasional visit to Amiens, a city built for a hundred thousand, but at the time inhabited by only a few thousand of the more venturesome inhabitants, who had returned to open shops and restaurants for the British, Australian and American troops. On account of lack of competition, prices were extreme even for France in war-time. The great cathedral was piled high with sandbags to protect its precious sculptures, but it stood as always, the sentinel of the city, visible ten miles away as one approached. The Church Army Hut of the British forces afforded separate accomodations for enlisted men and officers, and I had the pleasure of afternoon tea once or twice with some of the latter. Amiens was an unsatisfactory place to shop, but my baggage had not been found and winter was coming on fast, so I had to replace some of my possessions at once at any prices that might be demanded.

Our mess held its formal celebration on November

17th, with Lieutenant Robert Bernstein, the French liaison officer, as the guest of honor because of his exact prediction of the date of the armistice when he had returned from a visit to Paris several weeks previously. Our mess, officers' mess number two of division headquarters, had an international character through his presence and that of Captain Jenkins of the British army, and a special tone of comradeship through the influence of the president of the mess, Major Joseph Farrell, the division disbursing officer. So for once we had the rare treat of turkey and wine, feeling that the occasion demanded it.

I felt little pleasure in the jollity of the evening, however. I had just received a letter that day telling me of the death of one of my twin babies of the flu; it had happened almost a month before, while I was on the lines and quite out of reach of any kind of word. The war, through its attendant epidemics, gathered its victims also from among the innocent, far from the scene of struggle. I felt then that my grief was but a part of the universal sacrifice. With all these other parents, whose older sons died at the front in actual fighting, or whose younger ones were caught denuded of medical protection at home, I hoped that all this sacrificial blood might bring an end to war. To-day that faith is harder and that consolation seems a mockery, for we seem to be preparing for another struggle even while children are dying of hunger in central Europe and massacres of helpless Jews are still not yet ended in the east. When I received the news I took a long walk amid the most peaceful scene I ever knew, up the tree-lined banks of the

Somme Canal, with the evening slowly coming on and the sun setting behind the stiff rows of poplars.

At last we were detached from the British Third Army and received orders to entrain for the American Embarkation Center (as it was later called) near Le Mans. Our headquarters there were in the village of Montfort, where we arrived on Thanksgiving Day and stayed for three weary months. Montfort le Routrou is a village of nine hundred people, with one long street which runs up the hill and down the other side. The hill is crowned with a typical village church and a really fine château, where the General made his headquarters. The tiny gray houses seemed all to date from the time of Henry of Navarre; my billet was a low cottage with stone walls over three feet thick, as though meant to stand a siege or to uphold a skyscraper. The floor was of stone, the grate large and fuel scarce, no artificial light available except candles. The bed alone was real luxury, a typical French bed, high, narrow and very soft—an indescribable treat to a man who had slept on everything from an army cot to a cellar floor.

The surrounding country was rolling, with charming, little hills and frequent knots of woods. The division, as we had known it on the British front, was housed in forty villages, widely scattered about the countryside, and our artillery, which had fought in the American sector, was contained by ten more, located near Laval about fifty miles away. The men lived chiefly in barns, as the houses were occupied by peasants, who needed their own rooms. As far as the enlisted men were concerned, living accomodations were better in partially ruined territory, where they could at least occupy the houses, such as they were. Because we were in a populous region, only smaller units could be billeted in a single village, which meant less access to places of amusement. The typical French village has no single room large enough for even a picture show, except the one place of assembly, the church; apparently the farmers and villagers have no amusements except drinking, dancing (in tiny, crowded rooms) and church attendance.

Such cheerless lives hardly suited the Americans. Often the men had to walk a mile or more to the nearest Y. M. C. A. canteen, and those were improvised on our arrival by our own divisional Y. M. C. A. staff, which we had been permitted to bring with us on the earnest request of the chaplains of the division. After our long sojourn in the area, we left a completely equipped series of canteens and amusement buildings for the following divisions. The nearest available place for light and warmth, out of the mud and chill, was usually the French café, and that was available only when the men had money.

The greatest handicap on any effort for the morale of the men at the outset was the uncertainty of our situation. We were semi-officially informed that our stay in the area would be for only a few weeks, and that no formal program of athletics, education or entertainment could be arranged. When life grows dreary and monotonous, as in the Embarkation Center, the chief diet of the soldier is such rumors of going home. In our case three orders were promulgated for our troop movement, only to be rescinded again while the wounded, sick and special small detachments went ahead.

Another difficult problem was the one of covering ground. At the front it had been easy because the division was concentrated for action and because of the constant stream of trucks with their readiness of access. Even in the Corbie area the division had been so crowded together that seven services would reach every man who wanted to attend one or to meet me. At the rear the division would be billeted in villages, scattered about over twenty miles of countryside; it was impossible to get from place to place without transportation, and that was very scarce. The army gave the chaplains more encouragement and friendship than actual facilities for work; the chaplains' corps was just making its position strong at the end of the war. Fortunately, the Jewish Welfare Board came to the rescue here. It procured Ford cars for the Jewish chaplains about the first of the year 1919, thus doubling their scope for work and making them the envy of all the chaplains in France.

My work became a matter of infinite details, with little opportunity for organization but plenty for day labor. I arranged as many services as possible, getting to the various units by train, side-car, or walking until I obtained my own machine for the purpose. These services, from one to ten a week, were arranged through the battalion chaplains as a rule, though sometimes I established connections with some of the Jewish boys or with the commanding officer, especially in cases of detached companies without any chaplain at hand. Every service had its share of requests for information, advice, assistance, even for errands, as the men had difficulty in getting to the city to have a watch repaired or in reaching divisional headquarters for information. Some men would want to know about brothers or friends who had been wounded. Many had difficulty with their allotments, in which case I worked through the army, Red Cross, and Jewish Welfare Board. Others wanted information about relatives in Poland or Roumania, or to be mustered out of service that they might join and assist their parents in eastern Europe; unfortunately, neither information nor help was possible during the time we were in France. Some men wished to remain for the Army of Occupation or other special service; far more were afraid they might be ordered to such service and wanted advice how to avoid it and return home as soon as possible. Citizenship papers, back pay, furloughs,—the requests were legion, and the chaplain had no difficulty in being useful.

Naturally, one of my tasks was to gather accurate statistics of the 65 Jewish boys in our division who had been killed, to find exactly where they were buried, have their graves all marked with the *Magen David*, the six-pointed star, and keep the list for the benefit of their families when I should return. I even made one trip to Tours to discuss the possibility of making such a list for the other divisions which came into the area, though the task was too complicated to carry out completely in any but my own. Often men were lost to view entirely when they went to hospital; sometimes it transpired months later that a certain man had died or been assigned to another unit or sent back to the States.

But little by little the facts all came to light. Even here humorous incidents would occur, such as the time when I read a list of dead from their unit at one battalion service, only to have one of the men on the list speak up: "Why, I'm not dead, Chaplain!" It transpired that this man had been wounded on the head in an advance and had been reported as dead by two comrades who had seen him fall. So I had him in my records as "killed in action—grave unknown," when he was actually in the hospital, recovering slowly but completely. If he had been returned from the hospital to another division, as was often the case, I might never have known his fate.

In spite of such conditions I found the exact graves of all but three of the men on my list, and in the entire division, with its almost 2,000 dead, only fifteen graves were unknown at the time we returned. This was largely due to the untiring efforts of Lieutenant Summerfield S. Curtiss, the Division Burial Officer, who was my room-mate in Corbie and with whose methods I became familiar at that time. With the coöperation of the various chaplains and line officers, he was able to inspect and certify to the valuables left by men killed in action, to record every grave, and in the few instances where both identification tags and personal acquaintances were lacking, to take the finger-prints of the men before burial and thus preserve the only remaining traces of identity.

At this time I had the opportunity of seeing our division reviewed by General Pershing. The review was held at the Belgian Camp near Le Mans in massed formation. The men marched by in heavy masses; the General bestowed decorations on over a hundred heroes, including six Jewish boys; at the end he gave the officers an informal talk, telling us of the special need that existed for keeping up morale during the tedious period of waiting to go home.

That very subject had been discussed only a few days before by the chaplains of the division, meeting with General O'Ryan for the purpose. Chaplains' meetings were frequent, under the call of the Senior Chaplain, Almon A. Jaynes, where we took up not only details, such as arrangement of services in the various units, but also the broader moral and educational problems. The General's interest in our work and our aims was evident in every word spoken at the meeting, especially his searching queries as to drunkenness, dissatisfaction, and remedies for such evils as we brought out.

The three months of waiting had been in many ways harder than the previous months of battle. Interest in our military purpose was gone; the men had few amusements and much work to fill in their time. We had very little athletic or educational effort; that was prevented by our constant expectation of an early departure. Mail service was often bad, especially for the men who had been transferred repeatedly. Pay was unreliable when a man had been transferred or sent to hospital and his records lost or mixed up. And the French winter is a rainy season, with occasional days of clear cold. No wonder that the soldiers were disgusted with France, war, army and everything else. In the midst of this growing irritation, their pet phrase became, "Little old U. S. A. is good enough for me."

The average soldier did not meet the better class of French people, only the peasants and the prostitutes of the towns. He had little taste for the wonderful architectural and historical treasures of the country; he could not speak the language beyond his elementary needs; and—one of his great objections—the French undeniably have poor plumbing and bathing facilities.

On the other hand, the French country people did not like our soldiers over much. The soldier of any nation was rather noisy, rather rough, and had no idea whatever of property values. He took anything he needed, simply "finding" it, the worst possible trait to thrifty French country people. Then, talking only a few words of French, the American naturally left out phrases like "monsieur" or "s'il vous plait," and he was considered to be ignorant of ordinary politeness, a wild Indian, the brother of the savages still supposed to be thronging our plains. A small minority of our men did penetrate into French life and grew to love it; a minority of the French made the acquaintance of Americans and came to respect them. Unfortunately, the two peoples were introduced to each other under most unfavorable circumstances.

These conditions, together with the constant flood of rumors, had the worst possible influence on the spirit of the men, which went down steadily from its magnificent power at the front, until the news of our actual orders to move toward Brest brought it suddenly up again. As the first division in the American Embarkation Center on the way home, we had to suffer for the later units, all of which had a program of athletics, entertainments and schools ready for them when they arrived. Working to build up the spirit of the men under the most discouraging circumstances, we received a powerful object lesson of the influences most destructive to morale.

The value of my work was at least doubled by the Ford touring car lent me by the Jewish Welfare Board. I received it on New Year's Day, 1919, in Paris and drove back to Le Mans, almost transfigured by the fact. My driver, assigned for the trip only, was splendid; I could stop for a brief view of the château and park at Versailles and the cathedral of Chartres; I knew that from that time on I could go from unit to unit so long as the machine stuck together and the army store of gasoline held out. With this car I was able to visit the artillery in the Laval area, about fifty miles from our headquarters, and conduct one service in each of their regiments. The artillery had not been on the British front at all, but on the American, so they had quite different adventures from ours. They had supported several other American infantry units in the St. Mihiel sector and north of Verdun, and had received mercifully few casualties compared with our infantrymen and engineers. The trip to them by car was unusually delightful, over smooth roads which the great army trucks had not yet ruined, through country where American soldiers were a rarity and the children would crowd the doorways to cheer us as we went by; over the gentle wooded hills of western France, with the trees hung with mistletoe; through the tiny gray villages, with their quaint Romanesque churches, many of them older than the great Gothic cathedrals of the north.

While in Paris on New Year, I enjoyed the rare treat of a family dinner at the home of my friend

Georges Lévy, an interpreter with our division. Through him and Lieutenant Bernstein I reached some sort of an impression of the state of French Jewry to-day. To tell the truth, neither I nor the average Jewish soldier received a very flattering impression. The shadow of the Dreyfus case seemed still to hang over the Jews of France. They feared to speak a word of Yiddish, which was often their only mode of communication with the American Jewish soldiers. One shopkeeper, asked whether he was a Jew, took the visitor far in the rear out of hearing of any possible customers before replying in the affirmative.

For one thing, except in Paris and the cities of eastern France, Jews exist only in very small groups. I have mentioned the four families of Nevers and the little synagogue of Tours, with its seventy-five seats. Le Mans possesses an old street named "Rue de la Juiverie," so that at one time there must have been enough Jews to need a Ghetto, but in 1919 Le Mans had only four resident Jewish families and one or two more of refugees from the occupied territory.

Another menace to the loyalty of Jews is the general difficulty of all religious liberalism in France. Religion to most people in France means orthodoxy, Jewish and Catholic; this naturally suits only those of conservative background or temperament. Almost the only other movement is irreligious in literature, art, government and philosophy. Those large groups of liberals who in America would be adherents of liberal movements, Jewish or Christian, in France are usually entirely alienated from religion. The liberals are intelligent but weak in num-

bers. As a converse of this, the synagogue is largely
content with past glories, making little effort to ad-
just itself either in thought or organization to the
conditions of the time. The American Jews were
always interested to hear about the Jews of France,
of the greatness of Rashi in former days, and eager
to inquire about the present status. They never
could quite understand the condition of a country
where the government had been divided for years
by a pro and anti-Jewish issue, as was the situation
at the time of the Dreyfus case. American democracy, even in the young and unskilled mind
of the average soldier, had no concept for anti-
Semitism.

When we knew finally that the division was on its
way home, I preferred a request through General
O'Ryan that I should go home with it. But G. H. Q.
Chaplains' Office could not grant my wish; there
were too few chaplains of all religions overseas; and
we Jews in particular needed every worker there.
I was detached and assigned to the Le Mans area,
under the senior chaplain of the American Embarkation Center. Naturally, I regretted deeply seeing
my old comrades go without me. I reported at Le
Mans, obtained fourteen days leave to the Riviera,
which had been due me for over two months, and
said good-by. The Twenty-Seventh was the first
division to reach the Embarkation Center, the first
to leave for home as a unit, and it finally paraded,
without its Jewish chaplain, up Fifth Avenue to a
tremendous ovation. I studied the pictures several
weeks later in the New York papers, and actually
thought I saw the vacant place in the column where
I should have been.

CHAPTER V

WHEN I knew for certain that I was to remain in France I asked for my two weeks' leave and departed for the Riviera via Paris. It was my fourth visit to the metropolis, a city which grows only more wonderful at every view. Its boulevards and parks, public buildings and shops were always attractive; in addition, the art treasures were now beginning to come back to their places, and the crowds were taking on the gaiety of peace time in the brilliantly lighted streets, so different from the sober groups and dismal streets during the war. This trip carried me beyond to a land of myriad attractions and surpassing loveliness. The mediæval monuments of Avignon, the Roman antiquities of Arles and Nimes, the splendid modern city of Marseilles, Toulon with its quaint streets and charming harbor, Hyères of the palm trees, and on to Cannes, to Nice, that greater Atlantic City, Grasse with its flowers and perfumes, and Monte Carlo, garden spot of the whole—all blended in a mosaic whose brilliant colors can never fade. Overhanging mountains and sub-tropical sea together unite all the types of attraction of all beautiful lands the world over. The palms and flowers never seemed quite real to me, while one was quite bewildered by the works of man—ancient monuments, mediæval art, and the most modern trappings of contemporary play and luxury.

At Cannes I met Captain Limburg, in charge of the Motor Transportation Corps there, who helped me to reach the officers' convalescent hospital at Hyères to search for a friend. The trip of eighty-five miles by sidecar was the bright particular spot in the whole gorgeous festival of the Coast of Azure, up the heights of the Maritime Alps into the clouds and down again to the edge of the blue inland sea, past ruined castles of the Roman time and through the quaint southern villages of nowadays; ending finally at the hospital, which turned out to be the San Salvador, one of the most splendid winter hotels on the Mediterranean. I even heard Francis Macmillan, a captain in the intelligence corps, give a violin concert for the officers during my one evening there.

Nice and the surrounding territory were crowded by Americans, as it was the most popular leave area for the American army. The great casino on the pier was the Y. M. C. A. for enlisted men, while the officers had their club on the square. In fact, all the arrangements by the "Y" in the various leave areas were magnificent. This, probably its most successful single piece of work, has hardly received the attention it deserves. I found the same to be true of every leave area I visited, including Grenoble, where I stopped for a day among the Alps on my return trip. Altogether the brief fourteen days were one of those unforgettable experiences which linger in the memory. One of the fine achievements of the army was that it was able to give an experience such as this to many thousands of officers and enlisted men, for their own elevation and their greater knowledge of France.

I should like to emphasize, if I could, the importance of the leave areas for the morale of the troops and their better appreciation of France. During actual hostilities men were willing to give up their leave, especially Americans who could not visit their homes but wanted only a change. After the war, however, military discipline became constantly more irksome to the soldiers, and the week or two without orders, in a real hotel with sheets and table-cloths, sight-seeing or merely resting, was the one thing necessary to bring them back to their units content to work and wait till their turn came to go back home. It was also a rare opportunity to see the best side of France and the French, when they had seen only the worst. No soldier admired the France of the war zone, with its ruined villages, its waste stretches, and its shell holes. Neither did he care for the France of the rest areas, where he knew only the smallest villages, with the least attractive people to a young progressive from the western world. Now he was able to enjoy the beauty and luxury of that older and more sophisticated civilization which always considered him either an amiable savage or a spoiled child.

The trip back to Paris and Le Mans was an experience in itself. I met three young and congenial medical officers on the train, with whom I traveled the rest of the way, stopping off for a half day at the little known town of Digne in the Basse Alps, where we saw the ancient church with its crypt, the art gallery with its painters of local prominence, and the old Roman sulphur baths, still used to-day.

Another day at Grenoble brought us into the heart of the French Alps. We reveled in the city with the snow-caps about. I felt the usual thrill at the tomb of the Chevalier Bayard, and more than ordinary pleasure in the beauty of the city itself.

I now settled down at Le Mans for the work of the Embarkation Center. Le Mans is too well known to Americans who have recently been in France to require much description. It is a city of about 75,000 people, with the customary narrow streets in the heart of the town, the fine parks and boulevards of every French city, and the very interesting cathedral overlooking the whole. There are fragments of the old Roman walls of the third century, and as an ironic contrast a fine street running through a tunnel which is named after Wilbur Wright, whose decisive experiments in aërial navigation were carried on nearby. My billet was a pleasant home opposite the very lovely park, the English Gardens, and my landlady a tiny old gentlewoman, who used to bring me a French breakfast and a French newspaper every morning, and indulge in the most formal compliments, reminding me of a romance of the Third Empire. And for some time Le Mans was the center of 200,000 American troops on their way home!

Instead of one division to cover, I now had from three to six, varying as units came from their old locations and departed on their way to America. And if it had been impossible to cover one division thoroughly, in a great area such as this a chaplain could do only day labor. I traveled from one point to another, had a schedule of services almost every night of the week in a different camp, visited the transient divisions as they came in, and thus came into the intimate contact with the men by which alone I could be of use to them. The territory was an immense one, though much of the time I did not have to cover it alone. The 77th and 26th Divisions had Jewish chaplains while they were with us; Chaplain James G. Heller was associated with me until he was transferred to the Second Army (in fact, he was in Le Mans while I was still with the 27th), and after his departure Rabbi Reuben Kaufman of the J. W. B. was assigned to religious work under my direction. But even so the task was staggering. So many regiments and companies scattered over an area eighty miles long and sixty miles wide was no feasible proposition, even with the best of cars and a sergeant to drive it for me.

In addition to the billeting accommodations in every village, the area contained several large camps of importance. The Classification Camp, within the city, was an old French barracks turned over to our use, which housed a constantly changing stream of casuals and replacements, flowing from hospitals, camps and schools toward their various units. The Spur Camp held a large group of construction units, engineers and bakers. The Forwarding Camp was a replica of a training camp at home, and contained a division at a time, at first in training, later in transit toward the ports. The Belgian Camp, originally built for Belgian refugees, now had long rows of wooden barracks for soldiers, a huge and always busy rifle range, and special camps of various types, including one for venereal patients, who underwent a mixture of medical treatment and discipline.

The purpose of the Embarkation Center was to provide a stopping place on the way to the busy ports of Brest and St. Nazaire, where the men might be deloused, have fresh clothing and equipment issued to them, undergo thorough inspections of every kind, and in all ways be divested of the effects of war and prepared to return to America. This task usually took a month or more, but sometimes a division had been partially equipped in its former area and if the ships happened to be ready it might stay in our area less than a week. On the other hand, it might not pass the various inspections at once, or at the time the transportation home might be lacking, and hence its departure would be delayed time and again. This uncertainty of tenure made all work very difficult, especially work such as the chaplains' which depended entirely on personal contact.

The problem of these divisions, as of the 27th, was chiefly to preserve the splendid morale of the front while the men were in the dreary tedium of waiting. This was done by cutting down the drill to an hour a day, which made enough work in addition to the delousing, inspecting and other necessary activities. The rest of the time was devoted to athletics, an educational program, and a great amount of entertainment, all three under the Welfare Officer appointed by the commanding general of the Embarkation Area, while all the welfare agencies contributed to these various ends under his general supervision. My work, of course, was directly under the Senior Chaplain, according to army regulation. And as the various units moved toward their goal more rapidly and more steadily, the need

for special efforts to keep up morale grew less.
Men keep up their own morale when they really
know they are going home; the difficulties had been
largely caused by the complete uncertainty and endless delays.

Such success as I had was due very largely to the
excellant coöperation of the Jewish Welfare
Board. Sergeant Charles Rivitz, who had charge of
the work in the area, was deeply interested in the
welfare of the boys and shared the resources of the
organization freely with me in my work. I had
always found this same attitude; the J. W. B. furnished me a car, an allowance for welfare work, an
office in its building, and offered its rooms for
services in the various camps. Where it had no
huts, I was accorded the same privilege by the
Y. M. C. A. Whenever its aid fell short, it was because it had no more to give. By this time Le Mans
had a large and active group of J. W. B. workers,
both men and girls, with their center in the city and
huts in many surrounding points. I found the
workers' mess the most friendly and pleasant in
the city, quite as congenial as the one at the Junior
Officers' Club, which I often frequented.

Even in the stress and turmoil of the Le Mans
area ("the madhouse," as the boys called it) striking or humorous personalities appeared from time
to time. There was Abie, the wandering musician,
a little Jew who had a gift for rag-time but no great
intelligence, military or otherwise. Abie had gone
to France with a replacement unit, was located
near Le Mans and spent his spare time playing for
the Y. M. C. A. and the officers' dances. When his
unit moved toward the front to be incorporated in

some fighting division, he stayed behind, not as a deserter, but to play the piano for the "outfits" that followed. He managed even to live at the local hotel by the tips they gave him. After that time he reported, giving his full story in detail, to every commanding officer who entered the village, always to be given enough to eat, but never accepted into any unit as he had no transfer from his original one. At last his story got abroad, he was brought in by the Criminal Investigation Department and investigated, only to prove the truth of his every word. So Abie, happy once more, was stationed in the Classification Camp and detailed to the Jewish Welfare Board as a pianist, improvising his rag-time adaptations of serious music and getting many privileges and a steady income for doing the work he enjoyed best.

A different sort of man was the soldier in a famous fighting division, who sought a private interview with me. It seems that in the advance on the St. Mihiel sector he had rescued a Torah, a scroll of the Law, from a burning synagogue. Throwing away the contents of his pack, he had wrapped the scroll up in the pack carrier instead, and carried it "over the top" three times since. Now he wanted permission to take it home to give to an orphan asylum in which his father was active. A soldier was not ordinarily allowed to take anything with him besides the regulation equipment and such small souvenirs as might occupy little room, but in this case a kindly colonel became interested and the Torah went to America with the company records.

The great event of my service in Le Mans was **our** Passover celebration on April 14th, 15th and

16th, 1919. The general order for Passover furloughs read:

"Where it will not interfere with the public service,
members of the Jewish faith serving with the American
Expeditionary Forces will be excused from all duty from
noon, April 14th, to midnight, April 16th, 1919, and,
where deemed practicable, granted passes to enable them
to observe the Passover in their customary manner."

Among the central points designated for Passover
leaves was Le Mans, and the Jewish Welfare
Board and I labored to arrange a full celebration for
the thousand Jewish soldiers who came in from
four different divisions. Quarters were provided
in the Classification Camp for all the men who did
not have the money or the previous arrangements
for hotel rooms, as well as full accommodations for
the Passover feast, the Seder. The Jewish Welfare
Board obtained full supplies of Matzoth, unleavened
bread, as well as Haggadoth, or special prayer books
for the Seder.

The spirit was as strong a contrast as possible
to that of my other great service at the fall holydays.
Among our congregation were two men from the
isolated post of military police at St. Calais, fifty
miles to the east, and five from among the students
at the University of Rennes, a hundred miles west.
We had a number of officers among us, while five
French families, several Jews in the horizon blue
of the French army, and two in the Russian uniform—labor battalions, since Russia had withdrawn from the war—worshiped beside us. And
when the crowd began to assemble, the first men
I saw were a group of engineers whom I had not

seen since Atonement Day, seven months before.
They were on the way home now, their presence
emphasizing more strongly than anything else the
change that had come to us and the world in the in-
tervening time. Again there were the meetings of
friends and brothers, but without the pang of part-
ing afterward. One of the most touching features
of the Seder was the large number of requests that
I should inquire whether Sergeant Levi or Private
Isaacs was present. Then how the whole gather-
ing would be electrified when a voice cried out,
"Here," and cousins or comrades who had not
known even of each other's safety were able to exchange festal greetings and rejoice together.

For the two and a half days' leave the Jewish
Welfare Board and I tried to keep the men busy,
with something for every taste. The full program
included a Seder, four services, a literary program,
a vaudeville show, a boxing exhibition, two dances
and a movie. All were well patronized, for the
soldier had a cultivated taste in diversion, especially after the armistice. But certainly the most
popular of all was the Seder. The soup with
matzah balls, the fish, in fact the entire menu made
them think of home. We held the dinner in an
army mess hall, standing at the breast-high tables.
The altar with two candles and the symbols of the
feast was at the center of the low-roofed unwalled
structure. Toward evening the rain, so typical of
winter in western France, ceased; the sun came out,
and its last level rays shown directly upon Rabbi
Kaufman and his little altar. It was a scene never
to be forgotten, a feast of deepest joy mingled with
solemnity. Afterward we adjourned to the Theatre

Municipale for a full religious service with a sermon. Two of the shows of the festival leave were too big for the hall of the Jewish Welfare Board, so we were offered the Y. D. Hut, the great auditorium of the Y. M. C. A., which had been named after the famous 26th Division. One of these entertainments was the last performance in France of the "Liberty Players" of the 77th Division, who were about to leave for the States that very week.

Finally my work in France drew to a close. On the first of May, 1919, I received the orders for which I had been hoping so long. I was to be relieved and sent home to America. Rabbis in the uniform of the Jewish Welfare Board were now at hand, the number of men in France was decreasing, and my request to be relieved could at last be granted. A final two days in Paris for a conference with the heads of the J. W. B., Chaplain Voorsanger and Colonel Harry Cutler, another day at Le Mans to turn my records and office over to Rabbis Kaufman and Leonard Rothstein, and then I was off to Brest. I had the special good fortune of being held in that busy and rather uninviting place for only four days and then finding passage assigned me on the slow but comfortable *Noordam,* of the Holland-American Line. My last duty in Brest was to conduct a funeral, in the absence of the post chaplain, of four sailors drowned in an accident just outside the harbor. We had a guard of honor, a bugler, all naval, and I had the rare experience of an army chaplain conducting a navy funeral, as well as of a rabbi burying four Christian boys.

We were at sea twelve days altogether, being delayed by a gale of three days and also by a call for aid, which took us a hundred miles out of our course without finding the sender of the message. We entered New York harbor late one evening, and anchored off Staten Island for the night. There was little sleep that night; the officers danced with the cabin passengers, while the men sang on the decks below. The next morning early every one was at the rail as we steamed in past the Statue of Liberty, which stood for so much to us now, for which we had longed so often, and which some of our company had never expected to see again. After the customary half day of formalities at the dock, we were directed to different camps for discharge according to our branches of the service. I reported at Camp Dix, New Jersey, where I was mustered out of service, receiving my honorable discharge on May 26th, 1919, eleven months from the date of my commission, nine of which were spent with the American Expeditionary Forces.

CHAPTER VI

THE JEWISH CHAPLAINS OVERSEAS

MY experiences, which were fairly typical throughout, showed clearly the great need for Jewish chaplains in the army overseas. Even my trip on leave to the Riviera was typical, showing the effect of release from discipline combined with a pleasure trip on thousands of our soldiers, most of whom needed it far more than I; for the privileges of a chaplain, just a little greater than those of most officers, certainly had prevented my morale falling as low as that of many of the enlisted men. The Jewish chaplain was not only a concession to the very considerable body of Jewish citizens who felt that they should be represented in the military organization as well as men of other faiths; he had a definite contribution to make to the moral and spiritual welfare of the forces. We had to conduct Jewish religious services for both holy-days and ordinary seasons, to assist the dying Jew, and to pray for him at his grave. We had to defend the Jewish boys in the rare cases of prejudice against them, or, what was just as important, to clear up such accusations when they were unfounded. We had to serve the special needs of the Jewish soldier, whatever they might be, at the same time that we did the chaplain's duty toward all soldiers with whom we might be thrown.

The American Expeditionary Forces never had sufficient chaplains at any time for the work that was planned for them. The proportion desired by the G. H. Q. Chaplains' Office and approved by the war department was one chaplain to every thousand men, or one to an infantry battalion, besides those assigned to administrative work as senior chaplains of divisions and areas, and the very large number detailed to hospitals. The total number of chaplains who went to France was 1285, just half the number needed by this program, and from this total we must subtract a considerable group of deaths, wounds and other casualties. The chaplains' corps was undermanned at all times,—we Jews were simply the most conspicuous example. Compared to the general proportion of one chaplain to every two thousand men, and the ideal one of a chaplain to every thousand, we had one chaplain to every eight thousand men, and those tremendous numbers were not even concentrated in a few units but scattered through every company, every battery, and every hospital ward in the army.

The British forces contained one Jewish chaplain for every army headquarters, or nine in all. I had the pleasure of meeting Rabbi Barnett, the chief Jewish chaplain in the B. E. F., although I never met his predecessor, Major Adler. Through their long experience and the coöperation of the Chief Rabbi of England, the English chaplains were well equipped with suitable prayerbooks and other material, which I obtained from one of them for the use of our men while I was on the British front. Still, even with their larger proportion of chaplains to the Jews in service, the lack of transportation facilities and the tremendous rush of war-time, especially at the front and in the hospitals, made their actual duties impossible of complete fulfillment.

To cover the enormous field before us was plainly impossible. The chaplain could only work day by day, clearing a little pathway ahead of him but never making an impression on the great jungle about. When I first reached France, I grew accustomed to the greeting: "Why, you're the first Jewish chaplain I've met in France!" That was hard enough then, but it grew harder when the same words were addressed me in Brest just before sailing and on shipboard on the way home. And yet it was inevitable that twelve chaplains could not meet personally the hundred thousand Jewish soldiers scattered through the two millions in the American uniform through the length and breadth of France. Under these circumstances we all feel a natural pride in the work accomplished against adverse conditions. I for one feel that we did all that twelve men similarly situated could possibly have done, and I gladly bring my personal tribute to those others, chaplains, welfare workers, officers, and enlisted men, whose coöperation doubled and trebled the actual extent and effectiveness of our work. This includes especially the Christian chaplains and welfare workers; their own field was great enough to take all their time and energy, but they were always ready to turn aside for a moment to lend a hand to us, in order that the labors of twelve men serving their faith in the great American army might not be quite futile.

The first of the Jewish chaplains to reach France

was Rabbi Elkan C. Voorsanger, who gave up his pulpit in St. Louis in April, 1917, to join the St. Louis Base Hospital as a private in the medical corps. As his hospital unit was the third to reach France in May, 1917, Rabbi Voorsanger was one of the first five hundred American soldiers in the American Expeditionary Forces. In the medical corps he rose from private to sergeant, gaining at the same time an intimate first-hand knowledge of the problems of the man in the ranks. When the bill was passed by Congress in November, 1917, ordering the appointment of chaplains of sects not at that time represented in the army, Rabbi Voorsanger was the first Jew commissioned under its provisions. He was examined by a special board appointed overseas by General Pershing at the direction of the Secretary of War; his commission was dated November 24th, 1917. In January 1918 he was assigned to the 41st Division and in March to Base Hospital 101 at St. Nazaire. While posted there he conducted his first important service overseas in Passover 1918, the first official Jewish service held in the A. E. F. He was assigned to the 77th Division in May 1918 on their arrival in France where he served with a most enviable record, receiving the Croix de Guerre and being recommended for the D. S. M. for exceptional courage and devotion to duty in time of danger. The midnight patrol on the banks of the Meuse, by which he won these honors, was both a courageous and a useful exploit. He was promoted to Senior Chaplain of his division with the rank of Captain, the only Jew so distinguished. Finally in April 1919, instead of accompanying his division home he resigned his commission to become the head of the overseas work of the Jewish Welfare Board. He returned to the United States in September 1919, after two and a half years with the American Expeditionary Forces. Since that time he has continued his self-sacrifice and his devotion to his people in the service of the Joint Distribution Committee for the Relief of Jews in eastern Europe. In 1920 and 1921 he conducted two relief units to Poland and carried on their life-saving work.

When I arrived in France, Chaplain Voorsanger was stationed at Chaumont for the time being, to take charge of the arrangements for the Jewish holydays of 1918. I have already described how these were carried out, by designating central points for services, getting in touch with the French rabbis and synagogue authorities and assigning the few American rabbis at hand to fill in the deficiencies.

I was the fifth Jewish chaplain to reach France. Those who preceded me were first Voorsanger and then Chaplains David Tannenbaum of the 82nd Division, Harry S. Davidowitz of the 78th and Louis I. Egelson of the 91st. All these men served at the front, as did also Chaplain Benjamin Friedman of the 77th Division, who took up the Jewish work of that unit when Chaplain Voorsanger was promoted to the Senior Chaplaincy. Chaplain Davidowitz was the only Jewish chaplain to be wounded, receiving severe injuries from shrapnel; these put him in the hospital for several months and occasioned his being sent back home, invalided, the first of us all. The others, in order of their arrival, were Chaplains Jacob Krohngold, of the 87th Division; Israel Bettan of the 26th Division; Harry Richmond, at the port of Bordeaux; Elias N. Rabinowitz, at Blois; Solomon

B. Freehof, at First Army Headquarters; and James G. Heller, at Le Mans. The last two left New York on the day following the armistice, so that on November eleventh, 1918, the Jews of America were represented overseas by just ten chaplains and two representatives of the Jewish Welfare Board, Rev. Dr. Hyman G. Enelow and Mr. John Goldhaar.

The twelve of us represented all three Jewish seminaries in this country, although the majority were naturally from the oldest, the Hebrew Union College at Cincinnati, where Rabbi Freehof was even a member of the faculty. We came from every section of the country, east, west and south, including Krohngold and myself from little towns in Kentucky and Richmond from Trinidad, Colorado. Rabbi Richmond had the unusual distinction of not claiming exemption in the draft as a minister. He therefore entered the service as a private and was promoted to the chaplaincy just before his division went overseas.

The chaplains who were commissioned before the armistice and served in the United States were thirteen in number; Rabbis Nathan E. Barasch, Harry W. Etteleson, Max Felshin, Samuel Fredman, Raphael Goldenstein, Abram Hirschberg, Morris S. Lazaron, Emil W. Leipziger, Julius A. Liebert, Abraham Nowak, Jerome Rosen, Leonard W. Rothstein, Israel J. Sarasohn. Three of them, Rabbis Rothstein, Felshin and Barasch, soon after resigned their commissions and came overseas as representatives of the Jewish Welfare Board. When the great need for morale agencies was realized after the armistice, the War Department refused to relax its prohibition against the transportation of more chaplains or other special branches of the service, but favored the passage of large numbers of welfare workers instead. Rabbi David Goldberg was the only Jewish chaplain in the navy, with the rank of Lieutenant, junior grade; he served at sea on the transport, President Grant.

We were almost all reassigned as our divisions left for home and as the need grew in various areas, especially in the base posts and the Army of Occupation. Chaplain Davidowitz was sent home wounded, and Friedman accompanied his own division back. Krohngold, Bettan, Heller and Freehof joined the Army of Occupation in the order named, although for a long time Rabbi Krohngold was the only Jewish chaplain there. Rabbi Egelson left his division for the port of St. Nazaire, Rabinowitz was transferred from Blois to St. Aignan, and I was left behind at Le Mans together with Heller, who shortly after was transferred to the Third Army in Germany. Tannenbaum while stationed at Bordeaux was also, by special arrangement, appointed as supervisor of the Jewish Welfare Board for that area; and Voorsanger was mustered out of service to become executive director of their overseas work. Rabbi Richmond alone held the same post to the very end of his overseas service.

As I have mentioned repeatedly in my personal narrative, so long as a man was assigned to one division he had some chance of establishing personal contacts with his men and doing effective work among them; as soon as he was assigned to an area, he had to spread himself thin over a wide expanse of territory and could cover it in only the most cursory fashion. The problem was larger than the

matter of transportation, although that was serious
enough. The larger aspect lay in the number of
men, the number of companies, the infinite possibility of individual service if one were only able to
know all these soldiers personally, to understand
their needs, and to minister to them. Every hospital ward with its forty beds presented forty distinct individual problems,—often, indeed, more than
forty. Sometimes the same man would need pay,
mail, home allotment, reading matter, and contact
with his original unit and comrades. With the constant shifting to other hospitals further from the
front and then to convalescent camps, the ward
would always contain a new forty men and the
work was always beginning over again. This situation was not in the least unique. The hospital
simply represents the extreme case of what was true
in a less degree in every branch of the service and
every unit.

During the post-armistice period I had several
very agreeable reunions with my fellow chaplains,
which were at the same time valuable for our
common information and coöperation. At my very
first visit to Le Mans, on December 6th, I quite
unexpectedly met Chaplains Freehof, Bettan, and
Heller, as well as Rabbi Enelow, who had just come
to the city for the dedication of the J. W. B. headquarters. I devoured their comparatively fresh
news from home as eagerly as Voorsanger had absorbed mine several months before, when he was already entering his second year in France. The
second time was on the last day of the year, when
I met Rabbis Friedman, Egelson and Rabinowitz in
Paris, all coming there as I did for the cars which

the J. W. B. had ready for us. At the same time Rabbis Martin Meyer of San Francisco and Abram Simon of Washington were in the city, both captains in the American Red Cross. Their six months of duty in France had just expired and they were then making ready for their return home. We all had dinner together at one of the famous Parisian restaurants and discussed war and peace, France, America and Israel, until the early closing laws of war-time sent us all out on the boulevards and home. Chaplain Egelson and I saw the New Year in together, first hearing "Romeo and Juliet" at the Opéra and then watching the mad crowds on the streets, headed always by American or Australian soldiers, the maddest of them all.

The most important meeting, however, was the one called by Chaplain Voorsanger for February 24th at the Paris headquarters of the Jewish Welfare Board. Six chaplains were present, Voorsanger, Tannenbaum, Richmond, Heller, Bettan and I, together with Mr. John Goldhaar of the J. W. B. Our chief object was to work out a program of cooperation with the J. W. B., our second, to discuss our personal methods for the benefit of our own work. Voorsanger was chairman; we decided to form a Jewish Chaplains' Association, which never developed afterward; and planned to hold another meeting soon, which owing to military exigencies, we never did. But we did adopt a program of cooperation with the J. W. B., which indicates the mutual dependency and the closeness of contact which were almost uniformly the case. Our program provided that the J. W. B. should submit to the chaplain the weekly report of the area in which he was stationed and should have relations with the military authorities through him. The chaplain, on the other hand, was to make suggestions to the worker in his area, and in exceptional cases to the Paris office and was to be in complete charge of all Jewish religious work in his area, although religious workers were personally responsible to their superior in the J. W. B. Finally, provision was made for frequent conferences between the chaplain and the J. W. B. worker in the same organization. This program was approved, not only nominally but also in spirit by all the Jewish chaplains and welfare workers throughout the A. E. F. I know that in Le Mans our contact was so close that Mr. Rivitz instructed his religious workers to report directly to me for assignment of services and other division of labor, and I included their work with mine in my weekly reports to my senior chaplain.

On my final visit to Paris at the end of April I found a host of Jewish celebrities gathered together in the interests if the Jewish Welfare Board, the Joint Distribution Committee for the relief of Jews in Eastern Europe, the American Jewish Committee, and the American Jewish Congress. At the office of the J. W. B., I had a farewell conference with Rabbi Voorsanger and Colonel Harry Cutler, giving them a summary of the latest situation in my area. Colonel Cutler was busy as chairman of the J. W. B., one of the American Jewish Congress delegates to the Peace Conference, and a member of the Joint Distribution Committee. I met my old friend, Rabbi Isaac Landman, who was reporting the Peace Conference for his paper, the American Hebrew, and he introduced me in turn to Miss Harriet Lowenstein, at that time the Paris purchasing agent of the Joint Distribution Committee, especially in the important work of buying supplies originally sent to Europe for the use of the American forces. I encountered also three of the active workers of American Jewry, sent to represent us before the Peace Conference in such matters as might concern the Jews; Judge Julian Mack, representing the American Jewish Congress; Dr. Cyrus Adler, for the American Jewish Committee; and Mr. Louis Marshall, a representative of both organizations. The two last were also active in the Jewish Welfare Board, and Dr. Adler, vice-chairman of the Board, took charge as the representative of the Board after Colonel Cutler's departure for the States. Even on the ship going home I met two Jewish workers, Rabbi B. Levinthal of the American Jewish Congress delegation and Mr. Morris Engelman, returning from his work in Holland for the Joint Distribution Committee. By that time world Jewry was fully aroused and its delegates were busy, both at the seat of the Peace Conference and in the lands of eastern Europe, where Jewish suffering was becoming daily more intense.

CHAPTER VII

THE Jewish Welfare Board in the United States
Army and Navy was the great authorized welfare agency to represent the Jews of America,
as the Young Men's Christian Association represented the Protestants and the Knights of Columbus
the Catholics. It was organized on April 9, 1917,
just three days after the declaration of war, and was
acknowledged by the Department of War as the official welfare body of the Jews in September, 1917.
It was not so much a new organization as a new
activity of a number of the leading Jewish organizations of the United States: the United Synagogue
of America, the Union of American Hebrew Congregations, the Central Conference of American Rabbis,
the Union of Orthodox Jewish Congregations, the
Agudath ha-Rabbonim, the Jewish Publication Society of America, the council of Y. M. H. and Kindred Associations, the Council of Jewish Women,
the Independent Order B'nai B'rith, the Jewish
Chautauqua Society, the Order Brith Abraham, the
National Federation of Temple Sisterhoods, the New
York Board of Jewish Ministers, the Independent
Order Brith Sholom, the Independent Order Brith
Abraham, and the Women's League of the United
Synagogue. In the camps and cantonments at home
it did a large and important piece of work, establish-

ing 490 representatives at 200 different posts and putting up 48 buildings for its work at various important points. This great field, however, is outside the scope of the present study, which can take up only the overseas activities of the J. W. B.

One home organization must be mentioned in this place, the Chaplains' Committee which made recommendations to the War Department for the appointment of Jewish chaplains. This was composed of representatives of the leading religious bodies of the country: for the Central Conference of American Rabbis, Dr. William Rosenau and Dr. Louis Grossman; the United Synagogue of America, Dr. Elias L. Solomon; Eastern Council of Reform Rabbis, Dr. Maurice H. Harris; the New York Board of Jewish Ministers, Dr. David de Sola Pool; the Union of Orthodox Jewish Congregations, Dr. Bernard Drachman; the Agudath ha-Rabbonim, Rabbi M. S. Margolies. Dr. Cyrus Adler, the Acting President of the Jewish Theological Seminary of America, was chairman of this committee. They had the task of reviewing the applications of one hundred and forty-nine rabbis, of whom thirty-four were recommended to the War Department and twenty-five were commissioned by the time the armistice put an end to more appointments. I have already given in some detail the story of the twelve of us who served in the A. E. F., while the other thirteen did their service in cantonments in the United States.

The Jewish Welfare Board began to take up the overseas problem as early as August, 1917, when Rabbi Voorsanger, then Sergeant in the Army Medical Corps, received a letter from Colonel Harry Cutler, asking for such information as he had at command and also how far he might be able to coöperate personally with the Jewish work. Some months later, after Voorsanger had been appointed chaplain he was again asked for information. This time he was in a position to give a great deal together with recommendations. A certain quantity of supplies was furnished him at once, but no welfare workers were sent until the overseas commission had made its investigation and report.

The overseas commission of the Jewish Welfare Board, consisting of Congressman Isaac N. Siegel, chairman, Rabbi H. G. Enelow, Rabbi Jacob Kohn, and Mr. John Goldhaar, secretary, went to France in July, 1918, and were the first friends I met when I reached Paris. Their general work was to study the nature and scope of the overseas field so as to make recommendations on their return; incidentally to this, they were to establish contact with kindred organizations and with the army, open headquarters, and coöperate with the chaplains in the field in the holyday services. They made their surveys during the summer by constant traveling and numerous interviews with officers and welfare workers as well as with Jews in the service. Congressman Siegel made a trip to General Pershing's headquarters and to the sector then occupied by the 77th Division, where Chaplain Voorsanger was taken into consultation regarding the problems ahead. The Congressman then returned to America, while Mr. Goldhaar was left as executive secretary pro tem of the Paris office and Rabbis Kohn and Enelow conducted holyday services at different points. Afterward Dr. Kohn also returned home, and Dr. Enelow devoted himself to field work, establishing welfare centers at various points. Later on, when the army educational program was undertaken, he became the J. W. B. representative on the faculty of the Army University at Beaune. Dr. Enelow was recommended for a chaplaincy by the J. W. B. Chaplains' Committee, but was among those prevented by the armistice from receiving the rank. Meanwhile he labored in any capacity at hand, for he was determined not to return to America while work remained to be done among the soldiers in France.

All this was entirely inadequate for the task at hand, as we all realized at the time. At that time the J. W. B. was functioning in the overseas forces, not as a separate entity, but through the Y. M. C. A. This naturally prevented the full expansion of its independent viewpoint or the direct contact with the army officials which alone could give it standing. The arrival of the overseas commission made some difference in this respect, but the J. W. B. was not fully recognized as one of the responsible overseas welfare organizations until Colonel Harry Cutler, its national chairman, had come to France and presented his case at General Pershing's headquarters. There were more than the usual difficulties with passports and visés, owing to the German or Austrian ancestry of some of the most desirable workers; this was finally overcome by the chairman of the Board vouching personally for the loyalty of every individual recommended. The selection was limited, as with all welfare organizations, to men not subject to draft. With these obstacles the difficulties proved for the time insuperable.

This situation made it impossible for the J. W. B. to undertake any independent work before the armistice. It could only support and assist the work already being done by chaplains and by the dozens of ready volunteers among the officers and enlisted men themselves. The early history of Jewish welfare work abroad is that of a scattered band of eager, self-sacrificing workers who gave up their own time to labor incessantly for the welfare of the Jewish men in the service. The first task was to acquaint the soldiers with the fact that there was a Jewish Welfare Board, even though its Paris staff consisted only of Mr. Goldhaar, one stenographer and one office boy. Advertisements in the *Stars and Stripes* and the Paris editions of American newspapers and correspondence with Jewish and non-Jewish chaplains, American, French and British, did the work. Letters began to pour in for supplies, advice, information, and a great correspondence school of welfare work began.

The center of this work was naturally the Paris club rooms, in connection with the office at 41 Boulevarde Haussman. Mr. John Goldhaar was in immediate charge of both, with a mountain of mail on his desk from every part of the A. E. F. and a constant crowd of doughboys outside in the club rooms. His indefatigable labors and his profound sympathy for the boys in the service won him thousands of friends through the length and breadth of the forces. He continued in this position, with its constantly growing duties, until Captain Voorsanger was appointed Overseas Director of the J. W. B., when Mr. Goldhaar was made Overseas Field Director and put in charge of the field work. His Medaille d'Honneur from the French government was earned by the hardest and most valuable kind of war work. Mr.

Goldhaar gathered about him in the Paris club rooms a group of American Jewesses and a few of their French coreligionists as an entertainment committee to make the boys feel at home. Every afternoon they served tea—a little thing in itself, but a big one to lonesome boys without a friend nearby. It meant much effort, too, on the part of the ladies themselves, especially their leaders, Mrs. Ralph Stern, Mrs. Zacharie Eudlitz, Mrs. Engelman and Mrs. Hertz. Some of them came from the suburbs every afternoon, rain or shine, to render this devoted service. Monsieur and Madame Henri Bodenheimer opened their hearts and their homes, both in Paris and Tours, to receive the Americans; every Friday evening saw their table crowded with lonesome "buck" privates, especially the ones whom other people would overlook. With the assistance of these same people hospital visitation was begun. A registration book in the office began to fill up with the names of Jewish soldiers and officers, and letters sent home recorded the fact of their visits and often established an important connection for the welfare of the men themselves.

At the same time, among the hundreds of letter-writers and visitors eager to do something, anything, for their fellow-soldiers, a few began to stand out here and there as effective and central workers. The soldiers were always ready to coöperate; I found that out from my first service at Nevers to my last at Le Mans. So it was only natural that far more of them volunteered for this work than I can possibly mention. I shall simply have to speak of a few outstanding names, and leave it to the imagination of the reader to multiply these ex-

amples many times. In Chaumont there was Field
Clerk A. S. Weisberger, formerly of Scranton, Pa.
"Sandy" Weisberger mimeographed a little newspaper, the "Junior Argus," for his fellow-soldiers
from Scranton; organized the Jewish soldiers at
G. H. Q. for services and sociability; and referred
any number of men to the Jewish Welfare Board
for such advice or assistance as it could give. He
was later mustered out of service to become a J. W.
B. worker and met his death most tragically by an
accident in the Paris headquarters, during the fes-
tivities of Passover week, 1919.

In Dijon there was a group, Major Jacob Jablons,
Medical Corps; Miss Bessie Spanner, a regular army
nurse; and Sergeant J. Howard Lichtenstein, of
Baker Co. 339. They organized hospital visiting in
the many hospital centers in that area, celebration of
the high holydays, Simchath Torah parties, and
group gatherings of all kinds. This work was spon-
taneous and needed only supplies of stationery,
prayerbooks and the like to make it completely effective, furnishing a fertile field for the welfare workers
when they opened their community center there. By
that time the two last were also in the service of the
Welfare Board, Miss Spanner in the unique position
of head of the women workers overseas. In Tours
the outstanding figure was Colonel Max R. Wainer,
at that time a Major. He gathered a group of active
workers among the soldiers, used the local synagogue
as a center, and organized a full welfare program, including Friday evening services and round table dis-
cussions, hospital visiting, and distribution of stationery and prayerbooks. I dropped in at Tours for
a day to arrange for the holyday services; the local

committee of soldiers saw that special meals were provided for the Jewish men; and the bills were paid by the Jewish Welfare Board.

In the Le Mans area, which before the armistice was used as a classification camp from which soldiers were sent as replacements to units in the field, the first Jewish work was started by Sergeant Charles S. Rivitz of Army Post Office 762 through the aid and assistance of his commanding officer, Lieutenant Willing of Cleveland. Lieutenant (later Captain) Willing, though a non-Jew, had taken a deep interest in the Jewish men in his unit while still in camp in the States and continued this interest to France. With the approval of Gen. Glenn, in command of the area, Rivitz was detailed to the Jewish Welfare Board under the supervision of the senior chaplain of the area and Capt. Willing. Sergeant Rivitz was not a social worker at all, but had one source of strength which made his good will effective. He was a soldier, had attained his sergeancy through force of personality; he knew what the soldiers wanted and insisted on giving it to them. He rented a château as a club house largely on his own responsibility, and the Jewish Welfare Board soon found that both the structure and his method of conducting it were excellent. His chief assistant was Corporal George Rooby, who after his discharge from the service volunteered for the first unit of the Joint Distribution Committee in Poland, and continued serving Jewry there.

In fighting units also the Jewish officers and enlisted men were early active in welfare work. Two officers occur to me whose work I saw personally; undoubtedly there were many others with the same sort

of interest.   Captain Leon Schwartz of the 123rd Infantry, 31st Division, was active from the outset in
his own division and the Le Mans area.   Later, during the time when the army was trying every means
to keep up the morale of the troops, and the temporary organization of "Comrades in Service" was being pushed through the G. H. Q. Chaplains' Office,
Captain Schwartz was assigned to this work as the
Jewish representative, and addressed hundreds of
gatherings of soldiers, together with the Catholic
and Protestant spokesmen for morale and comradeship.   In the 26th Division, the "Yankee Division,"
Captain Bernard I. Gorfinkle of the Judge Advocate's office was one of the first and most effective
Jewish workers in France.   Captain Gorfinkle organized an overseas branch of the New England
Y. M. H. A., deriving his first funds from the Young
Men's Hebrew Associations of New England.   Later, when the Jewish Welfare Board arrived, he
joined forces with its Paris office for the benefit of
his men.   Mr. Goldhaar tells how surprised he was
after the battle of Château Thierry to be highly com-
plimented for the work of the J. W. B. in marking
the Jewish graves.   Of course, at that time no such
work had yet been undertaken.   On investigation he
found that the graves of Jews of the 26th Division
who fell in action had been marked with a crude
Magen David by their comrades under the initiative
of Captain Gorfinkle.

Wherever a Jewish chaplain existed the Welfare
Board had a means of contact with the men.   And
here and there throughout the A. E. F., volunteers
sprang up, establishing their little groups and doing
their own work, large or small.   In the 42nd Divi-

sion, to cite only one more example, some of the boys
came together and held holyday services during the
actual campaign, and afterward instituted their own
hospital visiting.   But then came the armistice, and
at the same time the passport difficulty was disposed
of.   Workers began to come; new plans were being
issued daily by the army authorities; the whole viewpoint of the work was revolutionized and the facilities suddenly enlarged.

The determining factor was that troops were no
longer being scattered for training and fighting but
concentrated for their return home.   Hence the J.
W. B. centered its work on the American Embarkation Center and the base ports, established a line of
centers in the chief points of the Service of Supply,
and went with the Army of Occupation to Germany.
The last to be supplied with workers were some of
the combat divisions not in the organized areas.
Thus the work grew.   The club-house at Le Mans
was dedicated on November 28, 1918, in the presence
of Major General Glenn, with speeches by Dr. Enelow and the prefect of the Department of the Sarthe,
and a vaudeville show and refreshments to wind up
the evening.   Buildings were rented in the ports of
Brest, St. Nazaire, Bordeaux and Marseilles, and a
line of centers established across France, from Le
Mans on through Tours, St. Aignan, Gievres,
Bourges, Beaune, Is-sur-Tille, Dijon and Chaumont.
The headquarters for the Army of Occupation were
at Coblenz, where the B'nai B'rith Building was employed and seven huts established through the area.
Finally as workers continued coming, they were
assigned to seven of the combat divisions, staying
with them in their movements through France and

saying farewell only after the troops were embarked
for home. These divisions were the 5th, 6th, 7th,
29th, 33rd, 79th, and 81st. When Antwerp became
an important port for army supplies a center was
established there as well.

Altogether the Jewish Welfare Board employed
102 men and 76 women in 57 different centers in the
American Expeditionary Forces. Of this personnel,
24 men and one woman, Miss Spanner, were mustered out of the service for this purpose, while the
others were transported from the States. Of the
buildings, 23 were located in towns and were rented;
the other 34 were provided by coöperation of other
organizations, 28 by the U. S Army, two by the
Knights of Columbus, two by the Red Cross, one by
the Y. M. C. A. and one by the Belgian Government.
In camps rough barracks or tents were usually the
thing; in cities the equipment varied, and in some
places was complete with kitchen, dance hall, writing
room, and offices.

I can speak of the large work in the Le Mans area
through personal acquaintance. There the personality of Mr. Rivitz was the decisive factor. With
his unerring knowledge of the soldier, he established
at once the policy of everything free, which was soon
adopted by the J. W. B. throughout its overseas
work. Religious services were provided, hot chocolate and cigarettes served, contact established with
thousands of soldiers for the personal needs which
they brought to the welfare worker. As the needs of
the area grew, other centers were established.
When the 77th Division, with its thousands of Jews,
was in the area, five huts were established in its various regiments and the men provided with every-

thing possible right at home. In other units where the Jews were more scattered, the centers were at the Division Headquarters. In cases where units stopped in our area for only a few days or a week, an automobile load of supplies with two workers was sent out on an extensive trip, meeting the boys and giving them as much personal cheer and physical sustenance as possible under the circumstances.

I have described this type of activity several times in connection with my own personal story. Here and there, however, special personalities or incidents stand out in the constant, exhausting labor to which the workers subjected themselves in the terrific rush of the morale agencies during that period of waiting to go home. In Germany at the head of the work was Mr. Leo Mielziner, son of the late Professor Moses Mielziner of the Hebrew Union College, a man of high reputation as an artist and of commanding personality. Mr. Mielziner, who had two sons in the service, conducted the work in the Army of Occupation with the finest spirit of fellow-feeling for the enlisted man. Under his direction the Jewish Welfare Board maintained such a high standard that when the Red Cross closed its railroad canteens in the occupied territory the J. W. B. was requested by the army to take them over.

At Gievres, where the great bakeries of the A. E. F. were located, the J. W. B. was the center for the bakery units. So when Purim came both Jews and non-Jews coöperated in baking a gigantic cake for the celebration. The cake, which had to be baked in sections, occupied not only the stage but also an addition made for the purpose. It was cut into 10,000 portions and every man in that camp received a slice.

As the crowning achievement of the A. E. F. bakeries, that Purim cake received a reputation of its own.

The Paris office, and still later the club rooms on Rue Clement Marot, were the entertainment center for the Paris district and all its many visitors. After its formal opening on Simchath Torah, every Sunday afternoon an entertainment was provided, with vaudeville, speeches or dancing, concluding with the famous chocolate layer cake made by volunteer workers among the American women living in Paris. The wounded were visited in the nearby hospitals and usually a group of convalescents was present in the front seats at the entertainment. The registrations in the big book served to unite many friends and brothers who had lost track of each other in the constantly moving wilderness of the A. E. F. A family wrote in from Kansas City that their son was complaining at not hearing from home; when the J. W. B. wrote him, it was his first news from home in his six months as a "casual" in France. Through the Paris office and the workers in the field the whole immense field of personal service and entertainment had to be covered, including much of the same work which was being done by the chaplains and in addition the furnishing of immense amounts of supplies which we and others could use up but could not provide.

During the high holydays the Paris clubrooms presented a remarkable mingling of Jewish soldiers of all the allied armies. Mixed with the olive drab and the navy blue of the United States were the Australians with their hats rakishly turned up on the side, the gray capes of the Italian, the French troops from

Morocco, the Russian in Cossack uniform, and a few Belgians. During Chanuka, which coincided with Thanksgiving in 1918, special services were held at the synagogue in the Rue de la Victoire, the largest in France. The synagogue was crowded with French men and women, all at a high pitch of enthusiasm, and with 350 American soldiers, the heroes of the occasion. The impressive service of the French rabbi was followed by a brilliant Thanksgiving sermon by Chaplain Voorsanger, who had been invited to come to Paris for the occasion. After services turkey and pumpkin pie were served at the club rooms, and while I was not there that day, I can testify that the pumpkin pie served at the Jewish Welfare Board on New Year's day, 1919, was one of the most poignant reminders of the United States during my stay abroad.

Due to the intense pressure of the situation, the actual volume of work done by the J. W. B. was surprisingly large. The entertainments and dances conducted at every center numbered fully 5,000, with an aggregate attendance of 2,750,000. Among the conspicuous units which toured the A. E. F. under Welfare Board auspices, was "Who Can Tell?" the Second Army show, which was underwritten by request of the Welfare Officer and was one of the most elaborate of the army musical comedies, with a full complement of chorus girls acted by husky doughboys; this production toured for five weeks and while in Paris was seen by President and Mrs. Wilson. There was the "Dovetail Troupe," a vaudeville unit which likewise went on tour. And there was the "Tuneful Trio," led by Mr. and Mrs. Henry Gideon of Boston, which came to France under the Y. M. C. A., and gave many excellent concerts under J. W. B. auspices; I heard one of their programs in Le Mans and felt not only the musical excellence of their work, but also the special appeal of their program of Yiddish folk songs to the Jewish men; this troupe delivered 81 concerts to fully 60,000 men. The army educational work received much support in the various huts, and two of the best equipped men in the J. W. B. service were assigned to it, Dr. H. G. Enelow for the University of Beaune, and Professor David Blondheim of Johns Hopkins, for a time executive director of the overseas work, for the Sorbonne in Paris. The bulk of the daily work in the huts throughout France appears from the fact that 2,500,000 letterheads were distributed and refreshments served without charge to a total of 3,000,000 men.

The records of religious work are equally imposing, as 1,740 services were held, with a total attendance of 180,000 men. The constant coöperation with the chaplains meant that far more than these were indirectly influenced and aided. Eighteen thousand prayer books were distributed and ten thousand Bibles. On Passover of 1919 the J. W. B. provided unleavened bread (matzoth), which had been furnished through the Quartermaster Corps, for the Jewish soldiers in the American forces, as well as for French and Russian soldiers. The J. W. B. even provided matzoth for six thousand Russian prisoners in Germany during Passover of 1919. At the request of the military officials, the Jewish Welfare Board took charge of welfare work for the sixty thousand Russian troops in France, who had come originally as fighting units, but after the withdrawal of Russia from the war had been transferred to agricultural labor. No other welfare agency had provided for them and so they were assigned to the J. W. B. which had a few workers who could speak Russian. It was rather ironical that these men in Cossack uniform, most of whom were non-Jews, received their only friendly service in France at the hands of the despised Jew.

The whole work of the J. W. B. abroad culminated in the Passover of 1919. The most intense moment for us chaplains had come during the high holydays when feeling was most profound and suspense at its deepest and when, in addition, we had to carry the burden almost unaided. By Passover the feeling had changed, the war was safely over, the men were rejoicing at their imminent return home, and we had the Jewish Welfare Board to arrange our celebration for us. Fully 30,000 of the Jews in the A. E. F. ate the Seder dinners furnished by the Welfare Board. I have already described our celebration at Le Mans, with its many features in which the J. W. B. and I worked together. A similar program was carried out everywhere. At Dijon Rabbi Schumacher of the local French synagogue, who had been most active throughout in the interest of the American soldiers, led a great congregation of 2,000 men through the rain to the synagogue for worship and afterward to the Seder tables. In Germany, the city of Coblenz became the leave area for soldiers of Jewish faith and was closed for all other furloughs during the three days. The Y. M. C. A. and the K. of C. assisted in giving proper honor to the Jewish festival and proper pleasures to the Jewish men, and with their aid boat rides on the Rhine, entertainments in the Festhalle, and all the features of a full amusement program were provided.

Most striking of all was the great Seder at Paris, with its crowd of American, Australian, English, French and Italian soldiers, some of them former prisoners in Germany, all of them united in the great occasion of their faith. Among the speakers and the guests of honor were some of the great leaders of Jewry, as well as personal representatives of Marshall Foch and General Pershing. Colonel Harry Cutler, Mr. Louis Marshall, Judge Julian Mack, Dr. Cyrus Adler, and Dr. Chaim Weitzmann were there, as well as many other celebrities. At that time and in that place the highest honor for any man was to worship and eat side by side with the soldiers, who had carried love of their country and loyalty to their faith to the last extreme of service and of sacrifice,

Decoration Day of 1919, which was observed by all France together with its American visitors, was another important ceremony for the Jewish Welfare Board, together with its French hosts at the great synagogue on the Rue de la Victoire. The sermon was delivered by Rabbi Voorsanger, the service read by Rabbi Lévy of Paris; and again the great throng of Americans in uniform and their French friends joined in the common worship of their faith and the common exaltation of their patriotism.

In addition to the overseas commission and the men in the field, several of the prominent officers of the Jewish Welfare Board went to France at various times and took personal part in the work. The first was Mr. Mortimer L. Schiff, who spent the months of December 1918 and January 1919 in France as a member of the commission of eleven of the United War Work Organization, which had just completed its great financial drive. In that capacity Mr. Schiff was equally interested in all the welfare agencies; naturally, he gave the full benefit of his advice to the J. W. B. In February 1919 Colonel Harry Cutler, chairman of the Jewish Welfare Board, came to France. Although burdened with duties for other organizations as well, he accomplished wonders for the work of the J. W. B. during his four months in France. His enthusiasm and vigor showed at once, as in any matter he ever undertook. He traveled throughout the A. E. F., observed conditions for himself, and then accomplished two important pieces of work. First he obtained an order from the General Headquarters releasing the J. W. B. from its former dependence on the Y. M. C. A. and allowing it to work directly in coöperation with the military authorities; this was certainly advisable under post-armistice conditions, and many others felt with me that it would have been the preferable system at all times. Second, he persuaded Chaplain Elkan C. Voorsanger, then completing his second year overseas, to allow his division to return home without him, while he stayed on from April to September as Overseas Director of the J. W. B. Together with Chaplain Voorsanger, Colonel Cutler administered the J. W. B. during the period of growth, and then left him to carry it on successfully during the time of retrenchment, until finally he also returned home with the Paris Staff, and the only representatives left in France were those working in coöperation with the Graves Registration Service.

Another important worker for the J. W. B. was Dr. Cyrus Adler, vice-chairman of the national organization, who reached France in March, 1919 as a representative of the American Jewish Committee. On Colonel Cutler's return in May, Dr. Adler took over his duties for the Welfare Board, and worked with Chaplain Voorsanger until the end of his mission, in July 1919.

One necessary part of the work of the Jewish Welfare Board, after all its efforts on behalf of the men in the service had been accomplished, was to care for the graves of those Jews who gave their all in the service of America. The Graves Registration Service, later called the Cemetarial Division of the War Department, had a great and necessary work. The Jewish Welfare Board obtained in February, 1918 a War Department order that all graves of Jews should be marked with the Magen David, the double triangle.

This order was confirmed by a response from General Pershing on July 29, 1918. Temporary Jewish headboards were supplied overseas, together with the temporary crosses, and whenever we knew definitely that a particular soldier had been a Jew they were used. Unfortunately, that information was not always available. Most units had no religious census, certainly none was up to date including the replacements. The order for marking the identification tag with an additional letter— "P" for Protestant, "C" for Catholic, and "H" for Hebrew—was issued after most of us were overseas, and hardly any of the tags had it; I know I never had the "H" put on mine. Often a man would carry a prayerbook in his pocket, but if the bodies were searched by one detail and buried by another that did not help. I know that it took me three months to verify my list of Jewish dead in the 27th Division, so that one can imagine the task for the entire A. E. F.

In May, 1919, the J. W. B. undertook this duty of identifying the Jewish graves, so that the War Department could mark them all properly. They have thus identified 1,500 altogether and where a cross had already been put up the headboard was changed. In this connection, a peculiar situation arose through the efforts of the Red Cross to photograph all graves in France for the benefit of the families at home. Such graves as had not been identified as Jewish still had the cross, and some families had their religious sensibilities shocked by the photographs. Hence the photographs in all such cases were detained until the changes had been carried out, and the Jewish Welfare Board had the graves photographed for the benefit of the families. Naturally, this work is being continued in the funerals of such soldiers as are being returned and in the care of such graves as shall remain permanently where our heroes fought and fell.

The sad death of Colonel Cutler occurred in England during the summer of 1920, on a trip which he undertook in the interest of the Graves Registration work, against the advice of his physicians and solely through his profound interest in the cause. His life was a sacrifice to his duty, to the tremendous efforts he had made for the Jewish Welfare Board and the other great national movements of Jewry. He gave, as so many others gave, another sacrifice for Judaism and America.

On the whole, the field workers of the Jewish Welfare Board made an enviable record in France.   In this respect a minor organization had the advantage in being able to choose its representatives so much more carefully than in the enormous machine of the Y. M. C. A.   The women workers were especially conspicuous for their steady, uncomplaining service. Their work was anything but romantic; it was driving, wearing labor.   They tended canteen all day and danced almost every evening, a régime that was hard physically and exhausting mentally.   Only those in the larger cities could enjoy the luxuries which are so commonplace in America—electric lights, a bath tub, and the other conveniences of civilization.   I have marveled to see them living for months in tiny French villages or in army camps, giving devoted service to the men in uniform, without distinction of rank or creed.

Through these workers the Jewish Welfare Board was able to render the personal touch which was missing in much of the war work overseas.   This applied especially to the Jewish man, who felt overjoyed to meet a Jewish girl from America, to attend a Seder, to write home on the J. W. B. letterhead.   He had found a touch of home in a foreign land; his personal needs could be understood and satisfied so much more easily and directly now.   But many men of many creeds found themselves at home in the J. W. B. huts.   Men learned to know Jews, to respect Judaism in the army who had been ignorant of both at home.   They often attended a Jewish service, met a Jewish chaplain, or simply preferred the home-like atmosphere to that of other welfare organizations.   For one thing, the J. W. B. was run according to the tastes of the soldiers; there was no charge for anything, even a nominal one; there was no condescension and no dictation, none of the things which the soldiers hated. In the Le Mans area, which was typical, from 56 to 60 per cent of the men patronizing the J. W. B. building were non-Jews. This constituted a return for the thousands of Jews who patronized Y. M. C. A. and K. of C. huts, as well as our contribution to the morale of the forces.

In some areas the Jewish Welfare Board was the most popular of all the welfare agencies; in all, it was very popular with the men of all faiths. The high caliber of the women workers, the personal touch and home-like spirit of the work, gave it a hold on the affections of the men. For a long time the Jewish soldiers had felt neglected by their own, not knowing the obstacles which had to be overcome. Then they found their own huts, suddenly springing up in all the central points, crowded and popular with all the groups of soldiers in America's composite army. The Jewish soldier became proud and the Christian soldier became appreciative. The excellence of the work brought forgiveness for every-thing, even though the soldier was not used to listening to reasons but formed his opinions quickly from the facts nearest at hand. The contribution through happiness and unity to the morale of the American Expeditionary Forces was one that did full justice to the eagerness and good will of the Jews of America.

CHAPTER VIII

THE JEW AS A SOLDIER

THE Jewish soldier demands no defense and needs no tribute. His deeds are written large in the history of every unit in the A. E. F.; they are preserved in the memory of his comrades of other races and other faiths. He was one with all American soldiers, for in the service men of every type and of every previous standpoint were much alike, under the same orders, holding the same ideals, with similar responses and similar accomplishments. The Jew was an American soldier— that really covers the story. For historical purposes, however, a further statement of numbers, honors, personalities, may be worth while. The Jew was in the American army, as in all the allied armies, because he exists among the population of every land. The studies made in various lands show that over 900,000 Jews fought in the World War altogether, of whom over 80,000 were killed in action or died of wounds. In the British forces casualties included the names of 8,600 Jews, and in the French forces, out of less than a hundred thousand Jewish population in the nation, 2,200 were killed in the service. These figures, picked practically at random from enormous masses of similar material, tend to show the participation of Jews in every army, just as they participate everywhere in the national life.

In the American forces the Jewish soldier ranked with the best; he was an American soldier, and there is no higher praise than that. With all the panegyrics on the American doughboy during and since the war, not enough has been said or can ever be said about him. His good humor, his self sacrifice, his heroism, won the affection and the admiration of every one. His officers loved him; his enemies respected him; his allies regarded him with mingled enthusiasm and patronage. They loved his youthful dash and were amused at his youthful unsophistication; at the same time they were profoundly grateful for his forgetfulness of self when the time for action came. I have mentioned some of the incidents in my own experience, illustrating the magnificent courage and abandon of Americans at the front—the youngster who came to the aid post seriously gassed but proud that he had stayed on duty the longest of any man in his company; the weary boys on the brow of a hill, digging in for the fourth time in a day of advances and fighting; the little Italian who stood on the edge of the shell hole that his comrades might advance—but the number and the variety of them was endless. Reading a list of the dry, official citations for decorations is like opening a mediæval romance of the deeds of knightly heroes. There was Captain Ireland who came to our aid post to have his wounds dressed and then started out without waiting for the ambulance. "Where are you going, Captain?" I asked. "Oh, back to the boys," was the answer, "I'm the only officer left in the battalion, and I don't want to leave them." There was the chaplain's orderly, himself a student for the ministry, who voluntarily organized a stretcher party to bring in some wounded men out beyond the barbed wire. Every type of heroism and self sacrifice existed, all carried off with the good humored bravado of school boys at a football game.

Among these heroes the Jewish soldiers were equal to the best, as their comrades and commanders were quick to recognize. A typical attitude toward them was that of a lieutenant colonel, telling me a story of his first battle, when we were on shipboard coming back home. "I was rather nervous about that first time under fire," he told me, "because I had a number of foreign boys in one company and didn't know how they might behave. Among them was a little Jew who was medical man of the company, carrying bandages instead of weapons, but going over the top with the others, a restless fellow, always breaking orders and getting into trouble of some kind or another. And when I came to that company on the front line the first thing I saw was that little Jew jumping out of a shell hole and starting for the rear as fast as he could run. I pulled my revolver, ready to shoot him rather than have an example of cowardice set for the rest. But I was surprised to see him turn aside suddenly and jump into another shell hole, and when I went over there I found him hard at work bandaging up another wounded soldier. He was simply doing his duty under fire, absolutely without sign of fear as he tended the boys who were hurt. I was sorry I had misjudged him so badly and watched his work after that, with the result that I was later able to recommend him for a decoration."

Ignorance, suspicion, ripening with knowledge

into understanding and admiration—that was the usual course of events. I quote Colonel Whittlesey, commander of the famous "Lost Battalion" of the 308th Infantry, a New York unit with a very large proportion of Jews: "As to the Jewish boys in the Battalion, I cannot recall many of them by name, but certain figures stand out simply because they are so unexpected. The ordinary run of soldiers, whether Jews, Irish, or Americans—the big, husky chaps who simply do what they are expected to do—naturally pass from our memory. It is the odd figures who stick in your mind. There was one chap for example (Herschkovitz was his name) who seemed the worst possible material from which to make soldier-stuff. He was thick-set, stupid looking, extremely foreign, thoroughly East Side, and yet, one day when we were holding the bank of the Vesle, and it became necessary to send runners to communicate with our commands, Herschovitz was the *only man* who volunteered for the job. It was a nasty physical job. It would have been a difficult thing if it had not been under fire, because it meant cutting through under-brush, up hill and down hill. Under fire this became almost impossible, and the boys knew it, so none of them cared for the job, but Herschkovitz made the trip four times that day. What was it? Well, just plain pluck, that's all. There were a great many fellows of this type—East Siders of whom the regular army men expected nothing at all—but the 77th Division just seemed equal to anything. . . ."

In the same unit was Private Abraham Krotoshinsky, who was awarded the D. S. C. for bearing the message which informed the division of the exact location of the unit, and was instrumental in releasing them.   Krotoshinsky was an immigrant boy, not yet a citizen, a barber by trade.   His own words give the story simply enough: "We began to be afraid the division had forgotten us or that they had given us up for dead.   We had to get a messenger through.   It meant almost certain death, we were all sure, because over a hundred and fifty men had gone away and never come back.   But it had to be done.   The morning of the fifth day they called for volunteers for courier.   I volunteered and was accepted.   I went because I thought I ought to. First of all I was lucky enough not to be wounded. Second, after five days of starving, I was stronger than many of my friends who were twice my size. You know a Jew finds strength to suffer.   Third, because I would just as soon die trying to help the others as in the 'pocket' of hunger and thirst.

"I got my orders and started.   I had to run about thirty feet in plain view of the Germans before I got into the forest.   They saw me when I got up and fired everything they had at me.   Then I had to crawl right through their lines.   They were looking for me everywhere.   I just moved along on my stomach, in the direction I was told, keeping my eyes open for them. . . .   It was almost six o'clock that night when I saw the American lines.   All that day I had been crawling or running doubled up after five days and nights without food and practically nothing to drink.   Then my real trouble began. I was coming from the direction of the German lines and my English is none too good.   I was afraid they would shoot me for a German before I could explain who I was. . . .   Then the Captain asked me who I was.   I told him I was from the Lost Battalion.

Then he asked me whether I could lead him back to the battalion. I said, 'Yes.' They gave me a bite to eat and something to drink and after a little rest I started back again with the command. I will never forget the scene when the relief came. The men were like crazy with joy."

In high position and in low the same kind of service came from the American Jew. This is the official citation of a Colonel, who is in civil life one of the prominent Jews of Chicago, Illinois:

"Colonel Abel Davis, 132nd Infantry. For extraordinary heroism in action near Consenvoye, France, October 9, 1918. Upon reaching its objective, after a difficult advance, involving two changes of directions, Colonel Davis's regiment was subjected to a determined enemy counterattack. Disregarding the heavy shell and machine-gun fire, Colonel Davis personally assumed command and by his fearless leadership and courage the enemy was driven back."

Judge Robert S. Marx of Cincinnati, Ohio, is now national president of the Disabled Veterans of the World War and a member of the national committee on hospitalization and vocational education of the American Legion. But in 1917 and '18 he was Captain Marx of the 90th Division, operations officer of his regiment during the St. Mihiel and Argonne offensives, and reported dead on the day before the armistice, when he was struck on the head and wounded severely. And at the other extreme, I notice the case of First Sergeant Sam Dreben of the 141st Infantry, a soldier of fortune in many revolutions and a member of the Regular Army in the Philippines several years ago. Discovering a party of Germans coming to the support of a dangerous machine-gun nest, Sergeant Dreben with thirty men charged the German position, killed forty of the enemy, took several prisoners, and captured five machine guns, returning to his own lines without losing a man. For this daring and important act he was awarded the D. S. C.

Of the various types of distinction emphasized during the war, all were as true of Jews as of any other group. Numerous cases exist where four or more members of a single family were in the service. There was the Fleshner family, of Springfield, Mass., from which four sons of an immigrant father and mother entered the service, the oldest of them only twenty-three. The oldest of these boys lost an arm and an eye while carrying ammunition through a barrage, but exclaimed later in the hospital: "I'm the luckiest Jew in the army. Any other man in my place would have been killed."

The New York Herald during the war described an indefatigable Red Cross worker, Mrs. Louis Rosenberg of North Bergen, N. J. This old Jewish mother had six sons in the service; the two oldest, each the father of two children, when summoned for the draft refused to claim exemption, and having invested their savings in two small notion stores, they left their wives in charge of them and accepted the call to military service. Mrs. Liba Goldstein, of Cambridge Springs, Pa., a woman of eighty-four, born in Russia, had twenty grandsons in the allied armies, ten as officers in the British army, eight in the American forces, and two with the Jewish Legion in Palestine. And so one might bring out one example after another, if one desired, all showing the eagerness of loyal Jews to serve their country.

The Office of Jewish War Records of the American Jewish Committee has made a remarkably interesting preliminary study of the number of Jews in the American forces. The office possesses 150,000 individual records, gathered by extensive coöperation with national and local Jewish organizations. The success of certain local efforts at intensive covering of the field indicate that the total number of American Jews in service during the war may amount to as many as 200,000. Of these about 40,000 came from New York City, 8,000 from Philadelphia and 5,000 from Chicago. Instead of their quota of three per cent., according to the proportion of Jews throughout the nation, the Jews in service actually constituted fully four per cent. of the men in the army and navy. The causes of this excess are not easy to establish. The draft may have been more fully enforced in cities than in many rural districts, and the bulk of the Jews are city dwellers. The proportion of young men among the various groups of our population would apply only if the Jews have more than their quota of young men, and we possess no facts to confirm that. But certainly the number of volunteers was an element in causing this large number of Jews in the service. The records show 40,000 volunteers among the Jewish men, practically one-fourth of the total Jewish contingent and a far higher record than that of the army as a whole.

In certain outstanding cases this record is even more conspicuous. The little colony of immigrant Jewish farmers at Woodbine, N. J., not over three hundred families altogether, contributed forty-three men to the service, of whom seventeen men, or forty per cent., were volunteers. Of the students at the rabbinical seminaries, who were all exempt by law, a conspicuously large number volunteered for service in the line, in addition to the chaplains among the graduates and the large number of both students and graduates who acted as representatives of the Jewish Welfare Board, lecturers in the training camps and similar capacities. In fact, the seminaries were almost empty for a year. Eleven students of the Hebrew Union College and four of the Jewish Theological Seminary waived exemption for regular service in the army and navy, including a number of men with very exceptional records. Jacob Marcus, now Rabbi and Instructor at the Hebrew Union College, volunteered in the Ohio National Guard and won his lieutenancy by brilliant work in the ranks. Three of the students there entered the Marine Corps during the first weeks of the war and served for over two years in that branch. One, Michael Aaronson, serving in the 31st Division overseas, was completely blinded while helping a wounded comrade in No Man's Land; now he is finishing his studies at the College with the same spirit which he showed in entering the service and in his work as a soldier.

The Jewish boys went into the army to fight. That appears in their proportion in the combatant branches of the American Expeditionary Forces. While these branches—Infantry, Artillery, Cavalry, Engineers, and Signal-Aviation—constituted 60 per cent. of the total, among the 114,000 records of Jewish soldiers in the hands of the War Records Office the distribution among these combatant branches is fully 75 per cent. The Infantry constituted 26.6 per cent. of the entire army, while among the Jewish records it constituted 48 per cent. Artillery was 14 per cent. of the United States army, 8 per cent. of the Jewish total. In cavalry the rate for the entire army was 2 per cent., for the Jews only 1.3 per cent. The engineer corps contributed 11 per cent. of the army strength, and but 3 per cent. among the Jewish records. The signal and aviation corps represented 7 per cent. of the United States total, and 15 per cent. of the Jewish total. The medical corps was 8 per cent. of the army total, 9 per cent. of the Jewish total. Ordnance was 1.7 per cent. of the army total, and 1.5 of the Jewish total. The quartermaster corps was 6.2 per cent. of the army total and 5.9 per cent. of the Jewish total.

The Army, Navy and Marine Corps altogether had nearly 10,000 Jews as commissioned officers, and a really tremendous number of non-commissioned officers. The Army records show more than a hundred colonels and lieutenant colonels of Jewish faith, including such distinguished officers as Colonel Abel Davis, whom I have already mentioned in connection with his D. S. C. for heroism displayed on October 9, 1918; Colonel Nathan Horowitz, of Boston, Mass. who spent 27 months in France in the heavy artillery; Colonel Samuel Frankenberger, of Charleston. W. Va., who commanded the 78th Field Artillery; Colonel Samuel J. Kopetzky, Medical Corps, of New York City, who commanded Sanitary Train 396, in the A. E. F.; and Colonel Max Robert Wainer, Quartermaster Corps, formerly of Delaware City, Del., who was awarded the Distinguished Service Medal and appointed a Chevalier of the Legion of Honor by the French government. These honors were but the climax to a military career that began with enlistment as a private in 1905, and promotion to the rank of Second Lieutenant in 1912. In the war every one of the four battles in which he took part was the occasion of a further promotion, so that he concluded the war as a Colonel. I have already mentioned Colonel Wainer in another connection, as the first active Jewish worker at Tours; as a matter of fact, he organized a Seder in his own unit in 1918, where 500 men celebrated the Passover at the same time that Chaplain Voorsanger was holding his Seder at St. Nazaire, and when practically no other Jewish work was being conducted in the entire overseas forces.

There were over 500 majors, 1,500 captains, and more than 6,000 lieutenants in the American army, with a full share of each in the A. E. F. Over 900 Jews were officers in the navy, the most conspicuous of them being Rear Admiral Joseph Strauss, in command of the mine laying work in the North Sea during the war. In addition there were one captain, five commanders and twelve lieutenant commanders. The marine corps included among its personnel over a hundred Jews as officers, among them three majors, one colonel, and Brigadier-General Charles Henry Laucheimer of Baltimore, Md., who died in January 1920.

The latest estimates of casualties run from 13,000 to 14,000, including about 2,800 who died in the service of America. This can be inferred easily from the branches of the service in which our Jewish boys were found, as well as from the number of honors they received. After all, for every brave man whose acts were noted and rewarded, many others just as heroic fought and bled unseen.

The number of Jews decorated for conspicuous courage is attested, not only by the Office of War Records, but also by the Jewish Valor Legion, an organization of American Jews who received such awards during the World War. Fully 1,100 citations for valor are on record. Of these, 723 were conferred by the American command, 287 by the French, 33 by the British, and 46 by other allied commands. The Distinguished Service Cross is worn by 150 American Jews, the French Medaille Militaire by four, and the Croix de Guerre by 174. The Congressional Medal of Honor, the rarest award in the American or any other service, which was conferred on only 78 men in the entire service, is worn by three American Jews, one of them killed in the act for which he was rewarded. I add their official citations, not only for their personal interest, but as an added tribute to these three heroes, a glory both to Jewry and to America.

"Sydney G. Gumpertz, first sergeant, Company E, 132nd Infantry. Congressional Medal of Honor for conspicuous gallantry and intrepidity above and beyond the call of duty in action with the enemy in the Bois de Forges, France, September 26, 1918. When the advancing line was held up by machine-gun fire, Sergeant Gumpertz left the platoon of which he was in command and started with two other soldiers through a heavy barrage toward the machine-gun nest. His two companions soon became casualties from a bursting shell, but Sergeant Gumpertz continued on alone in the face of direct fire from the machine-gun, jumped into the nest and silenced the gun, capturing nine of the crew. Awarded January 22, 1919."

"First Sergeant Benjamin Kaufman, Company K, 308th Infantry, Congressional Medal of Honor for conspicuous gallantry and intrepidity above and beyond the call of duty in action with the enemy in the Forest of Argonne, France, October 4, 1918. Sergeant Kaufman took out a patrol for the purpose of attacking an enemy machine-gun which had checked the advance of his company. Before reaching the gun he became separated from his patrol, and a machine-gun bullet shattered his right arm. Without hesitation he advanced on the gun alone, throwing grenades with his left hand and charging with an empty pistol, taking one prisoner and scattering the crew, bringing the gun and prisoner back to the first aid station. Awarded April 8, 1919."

"Sergeant William Sawelson, deceased, Company M, 312th Infantry, Congressional Medal of Honor awarded for conspicuous gallantry and intrepidity above and beyond the call of duty in action with the enemy at Grandpré, France, October 26, 1918. Hearing a wounded man in a shell-hole some distance away calling for water, Sergeant Sawelson upon his own initiative left shelter and crawled through heavy machine-gun fire to where the man lay, giving him what water he had in his own canteen. He then went back to his own shell-hole, obtained more water and was returning to the wounded man, when he was killed by a machine-gun bullet. Posthumously awarded January 10, 1919."

The 27th Division, in which I served, was fairly typical in this respect, as it was a National Guard unit, composed of volunteers from both the New York metropolitan district and "up-state." There

as further examples of the heroism of the Jewish soldiers in the American forces.

"Major Emanuel Goldstein, Medical Corps, 102nd Engineers. D. S. O., Belgian Order of the Crown. On Sept. 29, 1918, in the vicinity of Lompire and Guillemont Farm near Ronssoy, France, he remained in the most exposed positions under heavy shell fire and machine-gun fire, to render first aid to several wounded men, displaying exceptional bravery and courage, and setting a fine example of devotion to duty to all ranks."

"Second Lieutenant Samuel A. Brown Jr., 108th Infantry. D. S. C. awarded for extraordinary heroism in action near Ronssoy, France, Sept. 29, 1918. Advancing with his platoon through heavy fog and dense smoke and in the face of terrific fire which inflicted heavy casualties on his forces, Lieutenant Brown reached the wire in front of the main Hindenburg Line, and, after reconnoitering for gaps, assaulted the position and effected a foothold. Having been reënforced by another platoon, he organized a small force, and by bombing and trench fighting captured over a hundred prisoners. Repeated attacks throughout the day were repelled by his small force. He also succeeded in taking four field pieces, a large number of machine guns, anti-tank rifles, and other military property, at the same time keeping in subjection the prisoners he had taken."

"Corporal Abel J. Levine, Company A, 107th Infantry. For extraordinary heroism in action near Bony, France, Sept. 29, 1918. After his platoon had suffered heavy casualties and all the sergeants had been wounded, Corporal Levine collected the remaining effectives in his own and other units, formed a platoon and continued the advance. When his rifle was rendered useless he killed several of the enemy with his pistol. He was wounded shortly afterward, but he refused assistance until his men had been cared for and evacuated." Corporal Levine received the D. S. C. and the British D. C. M.

"Private Morris Silverberg, Company G, 108th Infantry. For extraordinary heroism in action near Ronssoy, France, Sept. 29, 1918. Private Silverberg, a stretcher bearer, displayed extreme courage by repeatedly leaving shelter and advancing over an area swept by machine-gun and shell fire to rescue wounded comrades. Hearing that his company commander had been wounded, he voluntarily went forward alone, and upon finding that his officer had been killed, brought back his body." Private Silverberg received both the D. S. C. and the British M. M.

One more point must be noted with regard to these Jewish boys who served America so bravely and so effectively. Many of them showed in their sacrifices the true Jewish spirit of Kiddush ha-Shem, sanctification of the name of God. Time and again have I heard men give such a turn to their speech, as when I asked a boy from one of our machine gun battalions why he had led a group of volunteers in bringing from an exposed position some wounded men of another regiment, an act in which the only other Jew in the company had been killed and for which my friend was later decorated. "Well, chaplain," he answered me, "there were only two Jewish boys in the company and we'd been kidded about it a little. We just wanted to show those fellows what a Jew could do." Dr. Enelow tells a similar story of a boy dying in a hospital, who gave the rabbi a last message to his parents, saying: "Tell them I did my duty as a soldier and brought honor to the Jewish name."

Once again, in the American forces during the World War, the Jew has proved himself a devoted patriot and a heroic soldier, and this time he has done so in broad daylight, before the eyes of all the world.

CHAPTER IX

JEW AND CHRISTIAN AT THE FRONT

TO those of us who served with the United States Army overseas, religious unity, cooperation between denominations, is more than a far-off ideal. We know under what circumstances and to what extent it is feasible, and just how it deepens and broadens the religious spirit in both chaplain and soldier. We have passed beyond the mutual tolerance of the older liberalism to the mutual helpfulness of the newer devoutness. Our common ground is no longer the irreducible minimum of doctrines which we share; it is the practical maximum of service which we can render together. I was in a critical position to experience this as the only Jewish chaplain in the Twenty-Seventh Division; my duty was to minister to the men of the Jewish faith throughout the various units of our division, with the friendly coöperation of the twenty other chaplains of various faiths. And I was able to do my work among the Jews, and to a certain extent among the Christians also, simply because these Protestant and Catholic chaplains were equally friendly and helpful to me and my scattered flock. Not by mutual tolerance but by mutual helpfulness were we able to serve together the thousands of soldiers who needed us all.

It is a commonplace that as men grow acquainted

they naturally learn to respect and to like one another. When a Jew from the East Side of New York, who had never known any Christian well except the corner policeman, and a Kentucky mountaineer, who had been reared with the idea that Jews have horns, were put into the same squad both of them were bound to be broadened by it. And, provided both of them were normal, average boys, as they were likely to be, they probably became "buddies" to the great advantage of both of them. Often such associations would bring about the sort of a friendship which death itself could not break.

One of the Jewish chaplains tells an incident of the first night he spent in the training camp at Camp Taylor, Ky. The candidate for chaplain in the cot next to his was a lanky backwoods preacher from one of the southern States. The two met, introduced themselves by name and denomination, and then prepared to "turn in" for the night. The rabbi noticed that his ministerial neighbor sat about, hesitated, and played for time generally, even though it was fully time to turn out the lights. Finally the matter became so obvious that he could not resist inquiring the reason for this delay. The answer came, a bit embarrassed but certainly frank enough: "I don't want to go to bed till I see how a Jew says his prayers."

On the whole, considering the many individual differences in an army of two million men, religious prejudice was not engendered by the army; some persisted in spite of it, and much was lessened by the comradeship and enforced intimacy of army life. In most commands prejudice against the Jew was a very small item indeed. It was so rare as to be almost non-existent in places of responsibility. It was often overcome by the acid test of battle when men appeared in their true colors and won respect for themselves alone. It was occasionally the fault of the man himself, who turned a personal matter into an accusation of anti-Semitism, and sometimes without cause. One Jewish corporal complained to me of discrimination on the part of his commanding officer, who had recommended his reduction to the ranks. On investigation, I found that the officer might have been unfair in his judgment, but had recommended the same for two non-Jews at the same time; the case may therefore have been one of personal dislike but was certainly not a matter of religious prejudice. When I found authentic cases of discrimination, they were usually in the case of some ignorant non-commissioned officer, who presumed on his scanty authority at the expense of some Jewish private. Or it might be a sort of hazing, when a group of ''rough necks'' selected a foreigner with a small command of English as the butt of their jokes. When men complain of prejudice against Jews in the army, it usually means that they met there a group of prejudiced people with whom they would not have come into contact in civil life. The tendency of the American army during the World War was definitely against prejudice of any kind; prejudice made against efficiency, and the higher one went the more difficult it became to find any traces of it.

In the army and especially in overseas service men went naturally to the nearest chaplain or welfare organization for any benefit except worship, and sometimes for that also. From my first religious service in a hospital with the crowd of non-Jews and sprinkling of Jews in the Red Cross room, I found that the men went to the entertainment hut for whatever it might offer. Every large service afterward, especially if held in a convenient place, included a proportion of non-Jews, and invariably they were both respectful and interested.

The burial work of the Twenty-Seventh Division at St. Souplet was the climax of coöperation among chaplains, where the five of us represented five different churches. Our service was a three-fold one, as was the later one held at the larger cemeteries at Bony and Guillemont Farm. I have already referred to the meetings held by the chaplains of our division to discuss our common work and arrange to do that work most effectively together. My very last duty in France was to read the burial service over four Christian sailors drowned outside Brest harbor.

Such incidents as these were not exceptional at the front or among men who have been at the front and have learned its lesson; I give them especially because they are typical. The men who were under fire together grew to overlook differences as barriers between man and man. They knew the many times that their lives depended on the courage and loyalty of the next man in the line—be he rich or poor, learned or ignorant, pious or infidel, virtuous or wicked. They grew to respect men for themselves, to serve them for themselves alone. The men used any stationery that came to hand, writing home indifferently on paper labeled Y. M. C. A. or K. of C., or Salvation Army, or Red Cross, or Jewish Welfare Board; they attended a picture show or boxing

match under any auspices and were willing to help
at any of the huts that served them. In the same
way the welfare workers and chaplains overlooked
one distinction after another, at the end serving
all alike and regarding their status as soldiers alone.
Once when I dropped into a strange camp two boys
whom I had never seen crowded through the press
of men in the Y. M. C. A. hut; they had seen the
insignia of the 27th, and being fresh from hospital,
appealed to me to help them back to the division
that they might return home with their own units.
I was never surprised when non-Jews came to me
for advice in ordinary cases, but I have had such extreme instances as a Jew and non-Jew coming
together, to ask advice in a case where both felt
they had been discriminated against by their commanding officer. In hospital work, in front line
service, even in the ordinary routine of the rest
area, we came closer to one another than ever in
civil life.

As I said above, the logical climax of friendly
coöperation comes when ministers of different faiths
assist each other in their own work. I shall never
forget a day in that busy October at the front when
I met a Baptist chaplain belonging to our division.
"Hello," he said, "I've just come to headquarters
here to look for you and a priest." "All right,
what can I do for you?" "Well," was his reply,
"our battalion goes into the line tonight, and I
wanted the Jewish and Catholic boys to have their
services, too. If you can come over at four o'clock,
I'll have the priest come at six." And so I came
there at four, to find the fifteen Jewish soldiers
grouped about a large tree near the battalion head-

quarters; the chaplain had notified them all. And, as the barn was both dirty and crowded, we held our little service under the tree, even though the rain began in the middle of it. Two of those boys did not come back three days later, and one was cited for heroism, so that I have often remembered the immeasurable service which the coöperation of that chaplain meant for his men.

On a minor scale such things took place constantly. One day, going to a distant battalion in a rest area, I not only went to the Y. M. C. A. man, who arranged for my services in the school-house, and to a Jewish corporal, who passed the word around to the men of my faith, but I arranged also that the "Y" man should conduct the Protestant service the following Sunday, and that the Catholic chaplain on coming should find arrangements made for his confessions and mass. A classic incident of the war is the story of Chief Rabbi Bloch, of Lyons, a chaplain in the French army, who met his death before Verdun in the early days of the war while holding a cross before a dying Catholic lad. The incident was related by the Catholic chaplain of the regiment, who saw it from a little distance. But by the time the gigantic struggle was over such incidents had become almost matters of everyday. I, for one, have read psalms at the bedside of dying Protestant soldiers. I have held the cross before a dying Catholic. I have recited the traditional confession with the dying Jew. We were all one in a very real sense.

A Christian chaplain preached the sermon on the second day of my Jewish New Year service in Nevers. Similarly, I was a guest, with the other members of the divisional staff, at the splendid midnight mass arranged by Father Kelley in the little village church of Montfort. For the first time in its history, the church was electrically lighted by our signal corps; the villagers and the soldiers were out in force; colonels assisted as acolytes; and the brilliant red and gold of the vestments, with the pink satin and white lace of the little choir boys, stood out brilliantly from the dark garments of the French and the olive drab of the Americans. Father Kelley delivered a sermon of profound inspiration, as well as a brief address in French to the villagers, whose guests we were. The staff were seated in a little chapel, at one side of the altar. The next day my orderly overheard two of the soldiers arguing about me. One insisted: "I did see the rabbi there right on the platform." "You didn't," said the other, "even if this is the army, they wouldn't let him on the platform at a Catholic mass." It reminded me of the incident in Paris when I had visited the Cathedral of Notre Dame, accompanied by my chauffeur, a Catholic boy, and I had given him a lecture on the architecture and symbolism of that splendid structure. It was only afterward that the humor of the situation struck me—a rabbi explaining a cathedral to a devout Catholic.

Every chaplain with whom I have compared notes has told me of similar experiences. Chaplain Elkan C. Voorsanger, for example, at the time when he conducted the first official Jewish service overseas at Passover 1918, received four other invitations in various sections of France both from army officials and Y. M. C. A. secretaries. At one point the Young Men's Christian Association even offered to pay all his expenses if his commanding officer would release him for the necessary time. I have mentioned that Rabbi Voorsanger had no regular services in the 77th Division during the fall holydays of 1918, due to the military situation. There was one exception to this, however, a hasty service arranged at one of the brief stops during the march by Father Dunne of the 306th Infantry, and that service arranged by a priest was conducted by the rabbi in a ruined Catholic church. Chaplain Voorsanger is full of praise for the thirty chaplains of various religions who worked under him when he was Senior Chaplain of the 77th. Their enthusiastic support as subordinates was fully equal to their hearty coöperation as equals.

Peculiarly enough, the Christian Science chaplain in our division was the only one who found it difficult to become adjusted with the rest. This could hardly have been personal, as he was generally respected. It may have been due in part to the general suspicion of some for the ministers of a new faith which had lured away a few of their adherents. But it seemed due chiefly to the ideas and the method he represented. He was handicapped for the necessary work of caring for the sick and wounded by a unique attitude toward physical suffering, different from the rest of us and different from that of most of the soldiers themselves. As a consequence he could serve most of them only as a layman might. Certainly he could give no religious treatment of disease, as the medical department was supreme in its own field. In addition, he could conduct general services only with difficulty. To the rest of us a service meant the same thing,—a psalm, a prayer, a talk, perhaps a song or two. But the Christian Scientist could not give a prayer. Prevented from using his ritual by the fact that the service was to be non-sectarian, he had not the power of personal prayer to fall back upon. He was not a minister in the same sense as the rest of us, and the army had no proper place for either a healer or a reader.

With this single exception, I feel certain that every chaplain in France had the same sort of experience. When I first arrived in France I was one of thirty-five chaplains assembled at the chaplains' headquarters for instruction and assignment. Our evening service was conducted in front of the quaint, angular château on a level lawn surrounded by straight rows of poplars. One evening Chaplain Paul Moody, of the Senior Chaplain's office, gave us an inspirational appeal derived from his own experience and his observation of so many successful chaplains at the front. Afterward, informally, a Catholic told us briefly what we should do in case we found a dying Catholic in the hospital or on the field, with no priest at hand. Then I was asked how best the others might minister to a Jewish soldier in extremity. I repeated to them the old Hebrew confession of faith; *Shema Yisroel adonoi elohenu adonoi echod,* "Hear O Israel, the Lord is our God, the Lord is One." I told them to lead the boy in reciting it, or if necessary just to say it for him, and the next morning when I brought down copies of the words for them all I was deeply touched by their eagerness to know them. These men did not go out to convert others to their own view of truth and life; they were ready to serve pious souls and to bring God's presence near to all. Christian ministers were eager to help Jews to be better Jews; rabbis were glad to help Christians to be better Christians. We learned amid the danger and the bitterness to serve God and man, not in opposition and not even in toleration, but in true helpfulness toward one another. I doubt whether these men, once so willing to serve men of all creeds at the risk of their lives, are foremost in the ranks of Jewish conversionists to-day.

Much of this spirit of genuine religion and of equal regard for all religions was due to the example and personal influence of the Senior Chaplain of the American Expeditionary Forces, Bishop Charles H. Brent, now the Protestant Episcopal Bishop of the Diocese of Western New York. Bishop Brent utilized his great ability, his high spirituality and his personal acquaintance with the Commander-in-Chief all for the welfare of the men in the service. Assiduous in his personal devotions, definite in his personal preaching, when he turned to his duties as Senior Chaplain he simply forgot his own affiliations in the interest of all religions alike. Catholic and Protestant had equal faith in the impartiality and justice of his acts. He was especially careful in behalf of the Jewish men because he knew that they were a minority and might otherwise be neglected. The official orders and the detailed arrangements for the various holydays were a serious consideration with him. His spirit animated his entire staff. Chaplain Voorsanger felt it from the outset. Chaplain Paul D. Moody, Bishop Brent's assistant in the chaplains' office at General Headquarters, was animated by it equally with his chief. Chaplain Moody, a son of the great evangelist and now in one of the important Presbyterian churches in New York City, was fond of telling how the various commanding officers would often greet him as "Father" or "Bishop."

It is hardly surprising that such coöperation strengthened men in loyalty to their own faith. As the soldiers saw the military rank of all the chaplains and their influence everywhere in the interests of the men, as they saw men of other faiths coming to their chaplain because of his loved personality or his high standing, as they saw the official bulletins announcing religious services of different faiths at different hours but under the same auspices, they grew to respect themselves and their own faith a little more. A young man is likely to be defiant or apologetic about being religious unless he sees religion, including *his* religion, respected by his comrades and his commanding officers. Therefore this mutual service, instead of weakening the religious consciousness of the various groups, rather strengthened it. Men grew to respect themselves more as they respected others more; they became stronger in their own faith as they became more understanding of others. The five chaplains at the burial detail did not give up their own ideas, but they did learn more about the others' faiths, and they certainly learned to respect each other profoundly as workers, as ministers and as men. Thus our mutual friendship and our mutual help became the foundation of all our efforts for the men, religious, personal and military. We did our work together as parts of one church, the United States Army.

This situation was brought out in strong relief

for me when I met in Le Mans a young French priest, who had served as chaplain in an army hospital through most of the war. He was overcome with astonishment when I told him that, while the majority of the men in our army were Protestant, the Senior Chaplain of the area at that time was a Catholic priest. I had to go into considerable detail, explaining that in some organizations the head was a Protestant, and in one division a Jew. Finally he grasped it, with the remark, *"C'est la liberté."* As a Frenchman it was hard for him to understand the kind of religious liberty which means coöperation and friendship. In France religious liberty is based on hostility and intolerance of religion. Religious liberty there means liberty for the irreligious and consequent limitation of the liberty of the religious. On the other hand, religion there has meant historically, the domination of one religion and the curtailment of liberty. It is a peculiar view, which is paralleled among French Jewry also. Active and interested Jews have little interest in modernism, even in modern methods of religious education; French Jews who are interested in the world to-day have little interest in Judaism.

We who served together in the United States Army have a different ideal. We think of a religion which gives equal freedom to all other types of piety, which works equally with men of every faith in the double cause of country and morality, which does not give up its own high faith but sees equally the common weal of all humanity, to be served by men of many faiths. We have fixed our gaze upon religion in action, and have found that the things which divide us are chiefly matters of theory, which do not impede our working effectively together. It needs but the same enthusiasm for the constant and increasing welfare of all God's creatures to carry unity in action of all religious liberals into the general life of America, to give us not merely religious toleration, but religious helpfulness.

CHAPTER X

THE RELIGION OF THE JEWISH SOLDIER

MUCH has been written of the soldier's religion, most of it consisting of theoretical treatises of how the soldier ought to feel and act, written by highly philosophic gentlemen in their studies at home or by journalistic travelers who had taken a hurried trip to France and enjoyed a brief view of the trenches. The soldier himself was inarticulate on the subject of his own soul and only the soldier really knew. Here and there one finds a genuine human document, like Donald Hankey's "Student in Arms," which gave the average reaction of a thinking man subjected to the trials and indignities of the private soldier in wartime, in words far above those the average soldier could have used. Theorizing about the soldier was worse than useless; it often brought results so directly opposite to the facts that the soldier himself would have been immensely amused to see them.

As a matter of fact, the soldier had the average mind and faith of the young American, with its grave lapses and its profound sources of power. He was characterized by inquiry rather than certainty, by desire rather than belief. His mind was restless, keen, eager; it had little background or stability. It was dominated by the mind of the mass, so that educated men had identical habits of mind with the ignorant on problems of army life. The moral standards of the soldier were a direct outgrowth of the morals of sport and business rather than those of the church. He had a sense of fair play, of dealing with men as men, but no feeling whatever of divine commandments or of universal law.

A significant incident, bringing out the peculiar ideals of the soldier, is related by Judge Ben Lindsey in his book, "The Doughboy's Religion." He tells how a number of Y. M. C. A. secretaries conducted questionnaires at various times as to what three sins the soldiers considered most serious and what three virtues the most important, hoping to elicit a reply that the most reprehensible sins were drink, gambling and sexual vice. But hardly a soldier mentioned these three. The men were practically unanimous in selecting as the most grievous sin, cowardice and the greatest virtue, courage; as second, selfishness and its correlative virtue, self-sacrifice; and as third, pride, the holier-than-thou attitude, with its virtue, modesty. The result, to one who knew the soldier, would have been a foregone conclusion.

The soldier was honest, he gave no cut-and-dried answers but his own full opinion, based upon the circumstances of his own life. At the front courage is actually the most important attribute of manhood and cowardice the unforgivable sin. One coward can at any moment imperil the lives of his entire unit by crying out in surprise on a night patrol, by deserting his post as sentinel or gas guard, by infecting with the spirit of panic the weaker men who follow any contagious example. Selfishness likewise was more than serious; it was vital. The selfish man was one who ate more than his share of the scanty rations on the march, who did not carry his full pack but had to be helped by others, who was first in line at the canteen but last to volunteer for disagreeable duty. Pride, on the other hand, was not dangerous but merely irritating in the extreme to an army of civilians, of Americans with the spirit of equal citizens, who felt that they were doing everything for their country and resented equally the autocratic and the patronizing manner. Besides the soldier saw examples of these, his highest virtues, about him constantly. Courage became a commonplace; self-sacrifice an every-day matter. Officers often shared the discomforts and exceeded the dangers of their men. When one reads the accounts of citations for the D. S. C. and Medal of Honor, one wonders that human beings could do such things. And when we who were at the front recall the utter democracy of those days, how salutes and formality of every kind were forgotten while only leadership based on personality could prevail, we realize anew the emphasis of the soldier on modesty and his resentment of the attitude of many a civilian and even a few military men in patronizing him either as a common soldier or as a miserable sinner.

As to religious tendencies, the soldier had, first and foremost, hope. He looked forward to better things both for himself and for the world. He had the religious longing and the religious certainty that the future will witness the dawning of a better day. He had a vast respect for manhood, though his democracy did not go so far as to include other nations, whom he very largely despised on account of their "queerness" and his own ignorance. He had an abiding hatred for anything which smacked in the slightest degree of hypocrisy or "bluff." I mention this in my next chapter in connection with preaching to soldiers, but preaching was not the only field in which it applied. The soldier laid an inordinate value upon personal participation in front line work, ignoring the orders which necessarily kept the major part of the A. E. F. in back area work, in supply, repair, or training duty. I know of one chaplain, for example, who joined a famous fighting division shortly after the armistice, through no fault of his own but because he had been previously detailed to other duty, and who found his service there full of obstacles through the suspicion of the men—because he who was preaching to them had not been under fire when they were. Of course, this worked favorably for those of us whom the boys had personally seen under fire at the first aid post or in the trenches.

This very respect for deeds and suspicion of words, especially of polite or eloquent words, made for suspicion of the churches and churchmen. We had so pitifully few chaplains to a division, and some of them were necessarily assigned to hospitals in the rear. Only here and there did a Y. M. C. A. or K. of C. secretary go with the men under fire. True, they had nothing to do there, as there was no canteen or entertainment hut at the front; true, strict orders forbade their entering certain territory or going over the top. The soldier asked not of orders or duties; he knew only that this man, who in many cases seemed to consider himself superior, who preached and taught and organized, had not slept night after night in the rain, had not fallen prone in the mud to dodge the flying missiles, had not lived on one cold meal a day or had to carry rations on his shoulder that he and his comrades might enjoy their scanty fare.

Therefore the soldier cared little for creeds of any kind. He could not apply any particular dogmas to the unique circumstances in which he found himself —he had probably never applied them to any great extent even in the more commonplace circumstances of peace—and he was suspicious of many of those who attempted to apply them for him. The soldier needed religion; he wanted God; he cared very little for churches, creeds or churchmen.

In most characteristics the Jewish soldier was one with his Christian brothers. He differed only in those special facts or ideas which showed a different home environment or a different tradition. For example, the usual Christian minister used the word, "atonement" with a special meaning which was understood, if not accepted, by every Christian present, but which meant nothing whatever to the Jew, except through the very different association with the Day of Atonement. So any analysis of the religion of the Christian soldier would begin with his attitude toward the atonement, but with the Jewish soldier this must be omitted—he had no attitude at all. The Jewish soldier was guided by the same general facts in his attitude toward the Jewish religion which animated the Christian soldier in his attitude toward the Christian religion; the difference was largely that of the religion which they considered rather than of the men themselves.

Of course, it was hard to be a good Jew in the army. The dietary laws were impossible of fulfillment, and the Talmudic permission to violate them in case of warfare meant less to the average soldier than the fact that he was breaking them. The Sabbath could not be kept at all, even in rest areas where there was no immediate danger to life. No soldier could disobey an order to work on the Sabbath; if the work was there, the soldier had to do it. In many ways Judaism was difficult and Christianity just as difficult. For example, I know of one division where the Passover service was held under difficulties, as the unit was about to move, and where the Easter service had the same handicap, as the men had just finished moving and were not yet established in their new quarters. Most of the obstacles to religious observance were common to all religions.

A few Jews denied or concealed their religion in the army as elsewhere. Some few enlisted under assumed names; a number denied their Judaism and avoided association with Jews, perhaps fearing the anti-Semitism which they had heard was rife in military circles. Their fear was groundless and their deception, as a rule, deceived nobody. The American army as it was organized during the war had no place for prejudice of any kind. Efficiency was the watchword; the best man was almost invariably promoted; in all my experience abroad I have never seen a clear case of anti-Semitism among higher officers and only seldom in the ranks. Occasionally also I met the type of Jew who admitted his origin but had no interest in his religion. Such a one—a lieutenant—who was known as a friend of the enlisted men generally and especially of the Jewish ones, assisted me greatly in arranging for the services for the fall holydays, but did not attend those services himself. He represented the type now fortunately becoming rarer in our colleges, the men who have too much pride to deny their origin but too little Jewish knowledge to benefit by it. It is noteworthy that this particular man was stationed in the S. O. S. and had at that time never been at the front. Most men turn toward religion under the stress of battle; those who have never been in battle presented in certain ways a civilian frame of mind.

Most of the Jews in the army were orthodox in background, rather than either reform or radical. Perhaps the orthodox did not have the numerical superiority they seemed to possess; in that case I saw them as the most interested group, the ones who came most gladly to meet the chaplain. Not that the other two groups were lacking in this army, which took in practically all the men of twenty-one to thirty-one years in America. The dominating group, however, was orthodox in background, though most of them were not orthodox in conviction. Causes are not far to seek—they had never studied orthodoxy; they were young men and had few settled religious convictions; they were in the midst of a modern world where other doctrines were more attractive. The fact is that their convictions were usually directed toward Zionism rather than toward one or another form of Judaism itself. Again, they were without reasons for their interest. Zionism appealed to them simply as a bold, manly, Jewish ideal; they did not enter into questions either of practicability or of desirability. In other words, they were young men, not especially thoughtful, who were interested in Jewish questions only as one of many phases of their lives. They had their own trend, but were glad to accept leadership of a certain type, adapted to their own lives and problems.

All these Jewish soldiers welcomed a Jewish chaplain. The Catholics and Protestants had chaplains, and all Jews except the negligible few who denied their faith were very glad to be represented also, to have their religion given official recognition in the army and to see their own chaplain working under the same authority and along the same lines as chaplains of other religions. Most of the Jewish soldiers had personal reasons also to greet a chaplain. In many of the occasions, small and great, when a Jewish soldier desired advice, aid or friendship, he preferred a Jewish chaplain to any other person. As a chaplain he had the influence to take up a case anywhere and the information as to procedure, while only a Jew can feel and respond to the special circumstances of the Jewish men. On the other hand, not all Jewish soldiers were eager to welcome the Jewish Welfare Board although they all liked it after it had arrived and made good. Some were afraid of any distinction in these semi-military welfare organizations, feeling that the two already in the field, the Y. M. C. A. and K. of C., were quite adequate. The Jewish Welfare Board, however, made such an impression at once on both Jews and non-Jews that even the doubtful ones became reconciled and felt that Jewish work in the army was more than justified by results. As always among Jews, who lay great emphasis on non-Jewish opinion, one of the chief causes of the popularity among Jews of Jewish war work was its popularity among Christians. When a Jewish boy found his building overcrowded by non-Jews, when he had to come early to get a seat at the picture show among all the Baptists and Catholics, when he saw Christian boys writing to their parents on J. W. B. stationery, he thought more of himself and his own organization. This same fact refuted the argument against segregation; men of all faiths used the J. W. B. huts, just as they did those of the other welfare organizations. They were one more facility for men of every religion, even though organized by Jews and conducted from a Jewish point of view.

In their religious services, as in most other things, the Jewish boys liked practices which reminded them of home. Just as many of them enjoyed a Yiddish story at an occasional literary evening, so they all appreciated the traditional Seder at Passover more than all the shows and entertainments which were provided at the Passover leave. They preferred to have many of the prayers in Hebrew, even though I seldom had a Jewish congregation in the army in which more than one third of the men understood the Hebrew prayers. They liked the home-like and familiar tone of the Jewish service on both Sabbaths and festivals. They preferred to wear their caps at service and to carry out the traditional custom in all minor matters.

But at the same time they had no objection to changes in traditional practice. The abbreviated prayerbook of the Jewish Welfare Board was much appreciated, even though one or two of the boys would state proudly that they had also a special festival prayerbook. The short service was practical and the boys therefore preferred it to the

longer one of the synagogue. They understood
that, with the large number of non-Jews at our
services and the usual majority of Jews who could
not read Hebrew, it was necessary to read part of
the prayers in English. They liked an English
sermon, too, although the chaplain skilled in army
methods always gave a very informal talk, far from
the formal sermon of the synagogue. And when
interested they asked questions, often interrupting
the even flow of the sermon but assisting the rabbi
and congregation to an understanding of the problem
at issue.

One of the chief characteristics of an army congregation was its constant desire to participate in
the service. The soldiers liked responsive readings;
they preferred sermons with the open forum
method; they were ready to volunteer to usher,
to announce the service throughout the unit, or for
any job from moving chairs to chanting the
service. At the Passover services at Le Mans,
we had all the volunteers necessary among
the crowd for everything from "K. P." (kitchen
police) to assist in preparing the dinner to an excellent reader for the prophetic portion. The services meant more to the soldiers as they became
their own.

Another characteristic of services in the army was
the large number of non-Jews attending them. I
have come to a Y. M. C. A. on a Sunday morning
directly after the Protestant chaplain, when most of
his congregation joined me, and my group in consequence was nine-tenths non-Jewish. At first this
factor was a source of embarrassment to many of the
Jewish men. They came to me beforehand to

whisper that a few non-Jews were present, but I took it as a matter of course, having learned my lesson with my first service in France. Later even the most self-conscious of Jews accepted the presence of non-Jews at a Jewish service just as Christians expect those of other denominations than their own. When Jewish services often have from ten to eighty per cent. of non-Jews in attendance, the Jewish soldiers are doubly glad to have a partially English service and a sermon. They want the Christians to respect their religion as they do their own, an end usually very easy of attainment. And while a few Jews would have preferred to drop the special Jewish characteristics of our service, I have never heard a critical word from a Christian about our wearing our hats, our Hebrew prayers, and the rest. Often, in fact, I have had to answer respectful questions, giving the sort of information which broadens both sides and makes for general tolerance.

At the front, even the most thoughtless desired some sort of a personal religion. In the midst of the constant danger to life and limb, seeing their comrades about them dead and wounded, with life reduced to the minimum of necessities and the few elemental problems, men were forced to think of the realities of life and death. With these eternal questions forced upon them, the great majority must always turn to religion. The men *prayed* at the front. They wanted safety and they felt the need of God. After a battle they were eager to offer thanks for their own safety and to say the memorial prayers for their friends who had just laid down their lives. Perhaps the most religious congregation I have ever had was the little group of men who gathered to-

gether under the trees after the great battle at the
Hindenburg Line. The impressions of the conflict
had not yet worn off. The men were, in a way, up-
lifted by their terrific experiences. And the words
they spoke there of their fallen comrades were infinitely touching. The appeal of a memorial prayer
was so profound in the army that many of the Protestant chaplains followed the Episcopal and Catholic custom and prayed for the dead although their
own churches do not generally follow the custom.　.

But with all this deep yearning for personal religion, the men adopted fatalism as their prevalent
philosophy. For one thing, it seemed to answer the
immediate facts the best. When five men are together in a shell hole and a bursting shell kills three
of them and leaves the two unharmed, all our
theories seem worthless. When one man, volunteering for a dangerous duty, comes back only slightly
gassed, while another left at headquarters is killed
at his dinner by long distance fire, men wonder.
And when they must face conditions like this day
after day, never knowing their own fate from minute
to minute, only sure that they are certain to be killed
if they stay at the front long enough, they become fa-
talists sooner or later. As the soldiers used to say,
"If my number isn't on that shell, it won't get me."
I argued against fatalism many times with the soldiers, but I found when it came my own turn to live
under fire day after day that a fatalistic attitude was
the most convenient for doing one's duty under the
constantly roaring menace, and I fear that—with
proper philosophic qualifications—for the time
being, I was as much of a fatalist as the rest.

At the rear the personal need for religion was less

in evidence.   The men who had gone through the fire were not untouched by the flame, and gave some evidence of it from time to time.   The men who had not been at the front, who comprised the majority in back areas, had no touch of that feeling.   They all shared in the yearning for home and the things of home and for Judaism as the religion of home, for the traditional service of the festivals, for the friendship, ministrations and assistance of the chaplain. Judaism meant more to them in a strange land, amid an alien people, living the hard and unlovely life of the common soldier, than it ever did at home when the *schul* was just around the corner and the careless youth had seldom entered it.   The lonely soldier longed for Judaism as the religion of home just as under fire he longed for comfort from the living God.   And the military approval of all religions on the same plane, the recognition by the non-Jewish authorities of his festivals and his services, gave Judaism a standing in his eyes which it had lacked when only the older people of his own family ever paid much attention to religion.   Thus Judaism as an institution, as the religion of home, had a great place in the heart of the soldier in France.

Some of the men, especially at the first, felt that they were being neglected by the Jews of America, that our effort was not commensurate with that which the Christian denominations were making to care for the soldiers of their faiths.   We must admit sadly that they had some justification for such a view.   Our representatives arrived in France late though not at all too late for splendid results. American Jewry was almost criminally slow in caring for our hundred thousand boys in service abroad. A few of the soldiers carried this complaint even to the point of bitterness and estrangement from Judaism. Here and there I met an enlisted man who challenged Jewry as negligent. Usually these were not our most loyal or interested Jews, but they were Jews and should not have been neglected. The men who entertained real loyalty to their faith were usually active already in some minor way and ready to coöperate with the Jewish Welfare Board when it was in a position to back them up. Most of the men, however, were eager to forgive as in a family quarrel as soon as our welfare workers arrived in France and showed immediate accomplishment.

Our Jewish boys came back from overseas with certain new knowledge of life and new valuation of their religion. Beginning merely as average young men in their twenties, they acquired the need and appreciation of their ancestral faith, though not in a conventional sense. They are not to-day reform Jews in the sense of adherents of a reform theology; neither are they orthodox in the sense of complete and consistent observance. They have felt the reality of certain truths in Judaism, the comfort it brings to the dying and the mourner, the touch of home when one celebrates the festivals in a foreign land, the real value of Jewish friends, a Jewish minister, a Jewish club to take the place of the home they missed over there. That is, Judaism means more to them both as a longing and an institution.

But not all the things which we customarily associate with Judaism have this appeal to them. Some seem to them matters of complete indifference, and the usual emphasis on the wrong thing makes them feel that the synagogue at home is out of sympathy with their new-found yearning. If we give them what we consider good for them, they will take nothing. If we give them what they want —the religion of God, of home, of service—and with all three terms defined as they have seen and felt them, then they will prove the great constructive force in the synagogue of to-morrow. The Jewish soldier had religion; if he was at the front, he has had the personal desire for God; in any case he has felt the longing for the religion of home. He was often proud of his fellow Jews, sometimes of his Judaism. He did heroic acts gladly, feeling the added impetus to do them because he must not disgrace the name of Jew. *Kiddush ha Shem,* sanctification of the name of God, was the impelling motive of many a wearer of the D. S. C., though he may never have heard the term. The recognition by church and synagogue of the world-shaking events of the war must be accompanied by an equal recognition of the influence of war on the minds and hearts of the men who engaged in it, and for whom those world-shaking events have become a part of their very being.

CHAPTER XI

PREACHING TO SOLDIERS

PREACHING to soldiers, as I soon learned, was a very different thing from addressing a civilian congregation. The very appearance of the group and place was odd to a minister from civil life—young men in olive drab, sitting on the rough benches of a welfare hut or grouped about in a comfortable circle on the grass of a French pasture. The group was homogeneous to an extent elsewhere impossible, as all were men, all were young, and all were engaged in the same work and had the same interests. The congregation and the preaching became specialized; the work became narrower but more directly applicable to the individual than in civil life. The soldiers had unusual experiences and interests as their common background; their needs were different from those of any group of civilians, in or out of a church or synagogue. They were soldiers and had to be understood and approached as such.

The circumstances of our services were never twice the same. I have led groups in worship in huts of the Y. M. C. A., K. of C., and J. W. B.; in châteaux, army offices, and barns; yes, and out of doors in the rain. I have come to a Y. M. C. A. and found it full, taking my group for an announced service to the stage and lowering the curtain for privacy. Once, in a great brick building used by the "Y," I found the place occupied by a miscellaneous crowd of a thousand men, reading, writing, playing checkers, lined up at the canteen for candy and cigarettes. My services had been announced and my fifty men were present, some of them after a five-mile walk. The secretary in charge and I walked about to find a vacant spot and finally found one, the prize ring. So I called for attention, announced my service, and held it in the prize ring, with my men seated on benches in the ring itself. The non-Jews near by stopped their reading or writing to listen to the little sermon, so that my actual audience was considerably larger than my group of worshipers.

I remember one week-day evening when I came to a J. W. B. hut in a camp near Le Mans for an announced service only to find the place packed to the doors. On inquiry, for such a crowd was unprecedented in this particular camp, I found that a minstrel show had been unexpectedly obtained and was to run later in the evening. So, while the actors were making up behind the curtain, I held forth in front, and when the show was announced as ready, a couple of Irish soldiers and a Swede pushed to one side and made a little room for me in the front row.

This very informality and friendliness of spirit meant, first of all, that one could not "preach" to soldiers in any case. They were intolerant of preaching. They did not want to be preached to. They wanted "straight goods, right from the shoulder." They wanted deeds more than words, or at least words which were simple and direct, of the force of deeds. One who knew soldiers had to *talk* to them, not preach. The more informal, the more direct, the more effective. A good sermon would often miss fire completely before an audience of soldiers when a good talk would wake them up and stir them. Informality, simplicity, knowledge of the soldier and his needs were the best qualities with which to approach the enlisted man, especially when he was or had been in the actual fighting and thus acquired a new sense of perspective. The strongest hatred of the fighting man was directed toward sham of whatever type, and he exerted that prejudice without any fine sense of discrimination against anything that seemed to him pretentious or hollow. The danger of pretense or dishonesty in the trench or on a patrol seemed to have entered into the whole mentality of the soldier. He distrusted the brilliant orator, who found more difficulty in winning him over than did the simpler and more direct type of speaker. He was certain to prick the bubble of a poseur at once, and was more than suspicious of anything which even hinted at pose or pretense.

For one thing, the material had to be concrete, the sort of thing the soldier knew. Jew and non-Jew were very nearly the same in the army, with certain minor differences of background. And hardly ever did one have an audience composed overwhelmingly of Jews; there was always a large admixture of others in any army audience, even when a Jewish service had been announced. Now, as to background and memories, our army was too mixed to rely on them for much material. When the chaplain spoke of home, the soldier might think of a tenement home or a ranch-house or a mountaineer's cottage. Certainly, only a few would ever have the same picture as the chaplain. When he 'spoke of foreigners, he might be addressing a group composed largely of Poles, Italians and Irish, who entertained very different ideas of what a foreigner might be, but would all consider our old Southern population, white and black, as foreign.

The only common ground of all soldiers was the army. The men knew work, discipline, war. They did not regard these things as an officer would, and a wise preacher found out their attitude in detail whenever he could. But this was concrete material, common to them all. They all hated to be under authority, but had nevertheless learned the lesson of discipline for practical purposes. They were fascinated by fighting, but feared it and preferred it, on the whole, to the tedium of peace. They found a greater monotony in army drill than in any other one thing in the world. They were brave when occasion arose. They had seen their friends drop dead beside them and had mourned and buried them. They had seen comrades promoted, now by favoritism, now by ability, and held a mixed feeling of ambition and of dislike for responsibility and the drudgery of thinking for themselves. They had problems of conduct, problems of morale, problems of vision, and they welcomed any discussion of their *own* problems in their own language, while despising infinitely the man who made a mistake in military terminology or showed lack of knowledge of the army. Their knowledge and their interest was narrow but keen, and one was compelled to meet the soldier on his own ground to interest or influence him.

This concrete material of the soldier's daily life had to be presented to him in his own language—minus the profanity which was all too common and meaningless in the average soldier's vocabulary. Here again the soldier proved a unique audience. With all his quickness to grasp an idea, his lightning sense of humor, his immediate sense of reality and recognition of fact, he had in many cases the vocabulary of a ten-year-old child. Many of our soldiers were from the mine, the farm, the sweatshop. Many of them learned English from the daily papers; many from their semi-literate companions. A few hundred very simple English words and plenty of army slang were the chief reliance of the preacher, and other expressions had to be defined as one went along. One did not need to "talk down" to the soldier in ideas—he could leap past a course of argument to a sure conclusion in any field within his experience—but the language was necessarily the language of the soldier for either full comprehension or complete sympathy.

Of course, the average soldier, Jew or non-Jew, had no homiletic background; he was not a frequent listener to sermons in civil life. In many cases the men admitted that they had never been in a church in their lives. Many of the Jewish boys had not been to a synagogue for years, and when they had gone many of them had attended an orthodox service where they had not understood a single word of the Hebrew service. Therefore the language of the Bible meant literally nothing to them without paraphrasing, except where it came very close to modern speech. Therefore also the cant phrases of the pulpit or of the public speaker generally had no meaning whatever to their minds, favorable or the reverse. They left the soldiers completely untouched. Thus the best civilian sermon may have been meaningless to a group of soldiers, while a direct talk, even a sort of conversation with the audience, was of real benefit to them. For there was no formality about an army audience. If one made the mildest joke, the boys laughed out. If one "paused for a reply," the reply was apt to come in loud and unmistakable tones. In a talk to a group about to return home, for example, I remarked, "I suppose you'll all reënlist in the National Guard when you get mustered out," only to be greeted by an immediate chorus of groans. If the soldiers were interested, they interrupted with questions; if uninterested, they frankly got up and left the room. They gave more than the cold decorum of a church; they gave a living response; they talked with and thought with the preacher. But the type of decorum one found in a church or temple was utterly beyond them. Their response was better, but different in its very activity.

Certainly, there were different audiences even among soldiers. I know of one preacher who traveled about France with a great speech on courage which fell utterly flat on a certain occasion. He had made the mistake of speaking on courage to a group of men from the Service of Supply, whose chief contribution to the war had been carrying cases of canned salmon and repairing roads. A certain chaplain had a battalion of recent immigrants mustered for a service before going into battle, only to be privately cursed afterward in the five languages spoken by the boys he had addressed. For he had made those boys give up their short period of rest to talk to them of home and mother, to make them think of the dear ones they were trying to forget, to put before them the one thought that was most likely to unnerve them for the terrible task ahead!

It was just as great a mistake to preach about sacrifice after a battle. In battle sacrifice was the most common thing; ordinary men rose to heights of heroism to save their "buddies" or to assist in the advance. The high courage of self-sacrifice became familiar. Preaching self-sacrifice to these men was useless—for Christian as well as Jew. They had seen stretcher bearers shot down while carrying their precious burdens to the rear. They had seen officers killed while getting their men under shelter. They had seen the gas guard, as a part of his daily duty, risk the most horrible of deaths in order to give the alarm for his comrades. Such men responded to an appeal on the divine in man, on the brotherhood of all those heroes about them, on Americanism, on a hundred congenial themes; they did not see the cogency of an appeal to sacrifice.

The profound friendships and violent dislikes of the soldier have been often noticed. His fidelity to his "buddy," to any popular officer, to his company and regiment, stand out as part of his vigorous, boyish outlook. On the other hand, a swiftly acquired prejudice would go with him forever in the face of many facts and much argument to the contrary. The relative standing of the Y. M. C. A. and the Salvation Army among the men is a case in point. The Young Men's Christian Association was by far the largest war work organization which worked among the mass of the soldiers, as the Red Cross confined its activities largely to hospitals and related fields. It was a wide-spread organization, covering practically every unit and almost every type of activity, religious, athletic, entertainment, canteen. But the soldier, while using the Y. M. C. A., disliked it. The Salvation Army, a very small organization in both amount and scope of work, which I never saw in action because I did not happen to be in the limited sector it covered, was, however, popular if only by hearsay in every part of the great army. Now, the soldier had very real grievances against the "Y." It charged him more for its tobacco than did the quartermaster's store; it gave away very little, while other organizations, not burdened with the canteen, gave away a great deal; it had a certain proportion of misfits, men who did not belong in any military work, who considered themselves better than the common soldier and did not share his trials or his viewpoint.

These facts were all explained later; some of them were inevitable. The presence of a board of inquiry in the army testified that the caliber even of army officers was not always what it should have been. The canteen had been undertaken by the Y. M. C. A. at the request of the army authorities, who desired to be relieved of the tremendous burden, and its prices were determined by cost plus transportation, which latter item was not included by the quartermaster's stores. The tremendous rush of the last six months of the war made the task too great for any of the organzations in the field, including sometimes even the quartermaster's corps. But after the prejudice had been conceived it could not be shaken. It persisted in spite of excuses, in spite of remedies for some of the evils, in spite of the excellent work which the Y. M. C. A. did in the leave areas. I have mentioned its activities in Nice, Monte Carlo, and Grenoble, how it provided the enlisted man with free entertainment,—excursions, dances and shows, during his entire period on leave. This striking contribution to the morale and the pleasure of the forces was almost overlooked in the general criticism. On the other hand, nobody ever heard the enthusiastic doughboy mention a mistake made by the more limited forces of the Salvation Army, which therefore received more than adequate commendation for its really effective work.

A similar violent contrast existed in the soldier's attitude toward the British and colonial soldiers, especially the Australians. The doughboy liked the "Ausies"; he despised the "Tommie." The usual phrase was: "Oh, well, the 'Tommies' are all right to hold the line, but it takes the 'Ausies' to make a push." This was strictly untrue, according to the terrific fighting we ourselves witnessed on the British front. It was simply that the Australians were all volunteers, young and dashing, like the pioneers of the western plains, the precursors of our own men. They were independent, lawless and aggressive. The British whom we knew were the survivors of four years of warfare, veterans of many a campaign in the field and siege in the hospital, or older men, the last draft of the manhood of Great

Britain. No wonder our boys liked the "Ausies" and refused to see any good whatever in that very different species of men, the "Tommies."

So the soldier was an exacting but a grateful audience. He emphasized deeds rather than words, and therefore he was much easier of approach for his own chaplain, who was under the same regulations as he, who went with him to the front and tended the wounded and the dead under fire, than for the most eloquent or the most illustrious of civilian preachers. He conceived violent likings and equally violent prejudices, always based upon some sort of reason but usually carried beyond a reasonable degree. He had to be approached on his own ground, with material from his own experience, with language which he could understand. And when that was done, he was the most thankful audience in the world. He thought with the speaker, responded to him, aided him. As an audience he was either the most friendly and helpful in the world or the most disappointing. But that depended on the speaker and the audience being in harmony, knowing and liking each other. A man who knew and loved the soldier could work with him and help him in achieving great results, for the American soldier, though the most terrible enemy, was also the best friend in the world.

CHAPTER XII

MORALE AND MORALS

NO thorough scientific study of the problem of morale has ever been made, in either military or civilian life. Every one is familiar with many of its manifestations, but very few have gone into their causes except incidentally to the practical needs of the moment. That was the case in the A. E. F., where both chaplains and line officers were deeply concerned in the morale of our troops, at first as fighting forces and after the armistice as citizens and representatives of América abroad. We tried this and that expedient, some good and some bad. Often we neglected the very act which was most essential. Often we did nothing whatever until it was too late. Unit commanders, chaplains, and even G. H. Q. were alike forced to employ empirical, trial-and-error methods instead of a fundamental, scientific approach. The only apology for this situation is that we went into the army with certain equipment which did not include a rounded view of mass psychology, and that this same ignorance is universal in civil life as well. A competent investigator would probably detect the same errors in similar social organizations of our young men in civil life which were so painfully obvious in the army. This brief chapter is by no means intended to take the place of such a scientific study; it may serve as material for one, and in addition may provide certain facts of importance in themselves.

Morale in the army represented two distinct problems, the front line and the rear. The former demanded high tension, the necessity of unified and instantaneous action. The latter demanded steadiness in daily duties, training, drill and study, the same qualities needed by the worker in civil life but under unusual circumstances. And between the two there was a gap, because the let-down from the one type of morale might result, not in the other type, but in no morale at all. The good soldier in camp might be a very poor soldier at the front, where different qualities were required; the man who would win his decoration at the front for reckless bravery was often the worst soldier in camp, judging by the number of punishments for the infraction of minor rules of discipline. There is the case, for example, of the former gunman who won his D. S. C. for the very qualities which had formerly sent him to prison. Even the best of soldiers, at both front and rear, had to withstand a serious mental shock when he passed from one of these situations to the other, and especially when he retired into a rest area after a hard spell in the trenches.

In the American army front-line morale was by far the easier type to maintain. In some other armies, I was told, the opposite was the case, but the average American boy makes a good fighting soldier with far less strain than it takes to turn him into a good barracks or training-camp soldier. His is the dash, the courage, the spirit of "Let's go!"; he is more likely to lack the sense of subordination, of instant obedience to orders, which constitutes the first essential of a good soldier in the rear. The object of morale at the front is action—instant, unified, aggressive, with every nerve and muscle strained to the utmost toward the one end. The means of this type of morale is confidence. The good soldier thinks that he belongs to the best company in the best division in any army in the world; that his officers are the ablest, his comrades the most loyal, his own soldierly qualities at least on a par with the best. Each division was firmly convinced that its own battles won the war, while the others merely helped, None of them would give the French and British credit for more than adequate assistance, ignoring completely their years of struggle before we even entered the conflict. But this sort of self-centered confidence was the characteristic of the good soldier, the man who would follow his captain in any attack, however desperate, who never looked whether his comrades were coming but went ahead in calm certainty that they would be even with him. One hint of wavering or doubt would break up this high steadiness of spirit, but as long as it held the men who possessed it would fight on in the face of seemingly insuperable difficulties.

I have mentioned the situation of the 27th Division from October 17th to 21st, 1918, how they entered the attack with depleted numbers, tired in body and mind, after insufficient rest and with no fresh replacements. Day after day their dearest wish was that their relief might come and they might enjoy the often promised rest. They had seen their comrades killed and wounded until a regiment had only the normal number of men to equip a company. Yet day after day the orders came for an advance, and every day those tired boys advanced. They did what we all considered impossible because they had the morale of good fighting men. They bore the ever-present danger of bursting shells and the sniper's bullet with boyish daring and constant success. They labored harder than any worker in civilian life, sleeping in the rain, marching, carrying their heavy rifles and packs made mercifully light for the occasion, digging in the clinging clay of the Somme valley. This, too, they did not gladly, often not willingly, but because it was part of the game, and they were good sportsmen and would see it through.

The peril to morale at the front was nerves. Although it may be hard to conceive, the dashing, aggressive soldiers might fall before this danger. Aggravated cases, true neuroses, we called "shell shock," slighter ones, "nerves," but the two were the same. The constant noise, exertion, hard work, loss of sleep, undernourishment, produced a peculiar mental state. Above all, the high nervous tension which was necessary for men to persist in these conditions had its dangers, too. By reason of it the wounded were able to bear more than their ordinary share of suffering, so that we saw constant examples of stoicism at the front. But when the excitement and tension wore off its effect was lost, and in base hospitals the soldiers were no better patients than young men in civilian life. When overburdened nerves gave way, the soldier was completely lost. A chaplain has told me of a long night spent with a patrol in front of the lines, not talking

with the men but instead trying to hold the top sergeant to his post. The sergeant was a fine soldier,
with a splendid record all through the Meuse-Ar-
gonne campaign, but that night, in the long vigil,
his nerves had given way and the big, stolid soldier
was trembling with fear. Only constant persuasion
and the threat of force held him to his duty, and the
next day he had to be assigned to work as supply
sergeant in order to save the nightly patrol from
panic that would certainly come if the non-com.
in command failed them.

The soldier had a mixed feeling toward battle.
The shock of conflict is exciting and exerts a sort
of fascination. But the excitement was short while
the danger was omnipresent and the work could
never be escaped. The soldier regarded war as
a sort of deadly game, where the contest called forth
every energy and the stakes were life itself. But
battle contains another factor—a compound of work
and discomfort. War is nine parts sordid labor
to one of glorious action. It was mixed with cooties,
mud, sleeping in the rain, marching all night and
lying down under artillery fire. It included digging,
and the soldier found no more romance in digging
in at the front than in digging a ditch at home, except that under fire he dug considerably faster.
War involved carrying a pack, and that became
speedily the pet hatred of the enlisted man. As
the prisoner dreads the cell in which he is confined,
so the infantryman feels toward his pack clinging
with its eighty-odd pounds as he trudges along
the weary roads. War is a glorious memory now,
but it was neither glorious nor pleasant to live
through.

When the troops retired for rest and training, the problem of morale became reversed at once. Now it became a matter of discipline and drill. Instead of danger and discomfort, our trials were work and monotony. A high type of morale in the rear meant that the men were not absent without leave, that they worked hard at their drill and became automatic in its motions, that they obeyed every rule of discipline, large and small. Saluting, for example, was very important at the rear; we never once thought of it at the front. This régime was not always easy, though at first we could hold out the object of winning the war, as in the pamphlet on sex education, "Fit to Fight." After the war was over that object no longer remained. But the hard work remained, the kitchen police, the cleaning up of quarters, the carrying of the pack, the incessant drill. "Squads east and west," when the fighting was at an end and there was no direct use for maneuvers, seemed to the soldiers simply made work. In fact, much of the work imposed on them during this period was actually devised with the special object of keeping them busy and therefore out of mischief.

The peril of this situation was obvious. It was that the tedium might grow too great and the men yield to the temptations of drink, gambling and vice. These would result in disorder, insubordination, time lost from duty, venereal disease,—any number of possible evils. They would demoralize a unit at the rear as readily as nerves would demoralize it at the front. Sexual vice and sexual disease, while statistically not so great in the army as among the same age groups in civil life, was still serious. The different social system of France put temptation directly in the way; prostitution was open and licensed, and the women of the streets quick to accost the wealthy foreigners, whose dollar a day was so much greater than the pay of the French soldier. At the same time, the French girls of good family did not meet strange soldiers, dance with them, talk to them, as was done in the States. Their whole conception of good breeding and of marriage combined to forbid any contact except in the rare case of a proper introduction into the French home. Courteous in showing the stranger his way or telling him the time of day, the average Frenchman was in no hurry to introduce foreign soldiers into his family circle unless he had certificates or personal introductions to the particular soldiers. At home the soldier had been lionized from the time of his enlistment until his leaving for overseas. He had been entertained, fed, provided with dances, shows and automobile rides. The daughters of rich and cultivated families tended canteen or danced with the soldiers. But in France the daughter of a good family went out only with a man she knew, and then strictly chaperoned. Even when she knew a man personally, a respectable girl would hardly think of walking down the street with him.

This seclusion of respectable French girls and the conspicuousness of the loose element made many soldiers hold a light opinion of the virtue of French women generally. I remember an argument with one of the boys who had just stated that all French girls were careless in their morals. When pinned down to particulars, he admitted that he had met exactly three French girls beside those who had accosted him on the street. Two had been sisters, at whose home a friend of his had been billeted, and when he and his friend had wanted to take them to an army vaudeville their mother had gone along. The third was the daughter of my landlady at Montfort, a fine rounded peasant type. On this scanty basis he had formed his typical opinions.

The control of the minutiae of daily life together with the influence over the minds of men in the army should have enabled the authorities to suppress vice almost entirely. Unfortunately, this was never accomplished. Lectures, severe penalties for disease "incurred not in line of duty," and liberal provision for "early treatment" all together did not work the miracle. The prophylactic stations for so-called "early treatment" directly after exposure were patronized by a number of men, but never by a very large proportion of the number who were certainly exposed. The venereal hospitals where sufferers underwent both treatment and punishment had their full quota from every division which remained long in back areas, and most divisions left behind as many as two hundred and fifty men for further treatment after the thorough inspections preceding their departure for home.

Drink was a less serious, though more prevalent danger. The law had prevented men in uniform from drinking in the United States; in France it forbade only their use of spirituous liquors, and even those were often available. So there was a good deal of beer and wine drinking, and some of cognac. The last was apt to result in drunkenness and disorder, but our military authorities had always the power to declare certain cafés, which had violated regulations, "out of bounds" for Americans, and as a last resort the French police would close such a place altogether. Gambling was the most prevalent vice of all, and one which was never, to my knowledge, controlled anywhere. It lacked gravity in so far as the soldiers had very little to gamble, and could incur no great losses. But it was always an easy resort to break the monotony of army life in training or rest areas, and always a menace to the type of manhood which we wanted to see among our American fighting men.

The reliance on penalties as the chief mode of controlling young Americans was fundamentally unsound both in theory and practice. The warnings against sexual vice lost half their effectiveness because they were usually given by company officers, who emphasized the danger of disease and the military penalties rather than the appeal of loyalty or self-respect. Medical officers and chaplains were certainly better equipped for such special work, although probably no human being and no appeal can solve the entire problem.

All these facts came slowly to the fore within the few months following the armistice, and we were able to observe them very clearly in the 27th Division while in the Montfort area. While we wintered there, from November 1918 to February 1919, the morale of our troops, which had never weakened at the front even under the most terrible conditions, went down steadily during those three weary months. For one thing, we were constantly expecting orders to leave for home and constantly disappointed. We were inspected and re-inspected, drilled and drilled again. Warned not to begin an elaborate program of athletics, education or amusement, we worked from week to week and never instituted one-third of the work which we had planned and ready. Meanwhile there was the café and the danger of vice and drink, so the men were kept drilling through the winter rains to keep them busy during the day and make them tired at night. This attempt was neither humane nor possible and had only the worst effects.

The failure with our division brought the possibility of a constructive program before the higher command of the army, which inaugurated one just about the time our division left the area. Large schools were started in each permanent division in the district, giving both common school and technical branches, with the army university at Beaune as the head of the educational structure. Such a school was established in the Forwarding Camp, near Le Mans, where I saw it in busy operation. Athletic meets were arranged in each division, with larger ones at Le Mans and other central points for the best men in the separate units. More welfare huts of different agencies were established, with more canteen supplies from the States and more women workers for canteen service and dances. Each division devoted more attention to its "shows," usually a musical comedy troupe, with very clever female impersonators to make up for the lack of chorus girls. Some of these shows had tours arranged by the Y. M. C. A. or other agency, and a few of them even had gala performances in Paris. Regular religious services and other appointments with the chaplains were instituted and advertised, although we had always done this for ourselves in our own units. Leave areas were designated in the most beautiful sections of France, as well as permission for a few furloughs in Italy and England. The *Stars and Stripes,* always a valuable organ as the soldiers' newspaper, became the constant instrument of propaganda to upbuild morale. Finally, the army took over official control of education, entertainment and athletics from the civilian agencies, designated a Welfare Officer to control them all, and asked the agencies formerly in control to coöperate with the newly appointed officials. All these were steps in the right direction, although at times such work was partially nullified by the choice of the wrong man as Welfare Officer. This was a position which only a professional educator could fill at all; even an expert could hardly influence actively a hundred thousand minds at once. Hardly any professional soldier, business man or engineer could have the breadth of view and technical knowledge to approach them. Of course, when army regulations prescribed a major for a particular position and only a lieutenant was available with the proper training, an untrained major was appointed and the lieutenant left in command of a platoon. Promotions were naturally few after the armistice, and the table of organization had to be complied with at all costs.

The *Stars and Stripes* demands a few words in itself, both because of its excellent articles and cartoons and for its unique position as "the soldiers' newspaper." It was a well-written weekly publication, which could command the services of many of the best of the younger writers and cartoonists in America. The knowledge that the *Stars and*

Stripes was semi-official, being published under military censorship, made its news material very influential on morale. Men believed anything they read there about the work of the various divisions, special distinctions, or the date of the homeward troop movement. But that very factor made the articles it published more or less suspected by the men. They knew they were propaganda, written for the benefit of morale, and they therefore read them, but derived much less effect from them than would otherwise have been the case. Still the writers, themselves soldiers, expressed the soldiers' view often enough and clearly enough to lend some value even to the suspected material from General Headquarters.

After all, amusements, education and athletics were only palliatives in a confessedly irksome situation. They did not touch the heart of that situation any more than really excellent welfare work satisfies a group of employees in civil life who consider themselves underpaid and overworked. The essentials of morale were the elements which approached the soldiers' welfare most nearly—food, pay, mail and daily military routine. Army food was notoriously bad, army cooks famous for lack of skill. Part of this, like other complaints, lay in the chronic grumbling of the soldiers. Obviously, they did not receive the kind of meals that "mother used to make" or the product of a famous hotel. The food itself was usually of excellent quality but coarse, the menus well balanced but monotonous. This last was the chief grievance and one that was largely justified. Most of our food had to be brought overseas in cans, and it took a skillful cook to disguise "corned willie," "monkeymeat" or "goldfish" day in and day out. Yet corned beef, stew and salmon, to use their civilian names, were staples in the army diet. It became a question among us officers whether we preferred to drink good coffee, ruined by army cooks, or the excellently prepared chicory of the usual French restaurant. I, for one, preferred the British ration as superior in variety to that we received after we came into the American area, although it was normally not as large in amount as the ration of the American soldier.

Pay and mail were notoriously unreliable in the A. E. F. Pay was regular for officers, of course, who could swear to their own pay vouchers, but not always for enlisted men, who required a service record to have their names put on the pay roll. When a man is a patient in nine hospitals within four months, we cannot expect his mail to follow him, nor his service record to stay at hand. These grievances were later remedied, the mail through the Main Post Office, the pay question by means of pay books and supplementary service records. Still, at one time it was by no means uncommon to meet men just out of the hospital who had received neither mail nor pay for three months, or to find a man who had been shifted so often from one unit to another that his pay was six months in arrears. When we remember the little money at hand for any purpose whatever, when we bear in mind the loneliness of these boys so far from home, loved ones, even from common sights and familiar speech, we can imagine what a deprivation such troubles brought, and how deeply they effected morale. Of course, as I have mentioned before, the soldier never made allowances either for the difficulty of the task or the comparative success with which it was accomplished. The soldier merely suffered and complained.

I shall never forget the incessant complaints about that very necessary institution, the censorship of letters home. The last hope of the soldier was for glory in the eyes of the people at home. At least he would be a hero to them. But here the censor lifted his terrible shears. Stories of heroism, true or false, could not be told. Weeks after an action the soldier's family might read that he had taken part in it and even then the censor might return his letter if he mentioned any details. For many of the soldiers this was more than annoying; it was serious. They were often not educated, had written perhaps three or four letters in their lives, and could hardly face the task of writing a second letter if the first was condemned. In any case no American wanted to submit his personal letters for his wife or sweetheart to a superior officer for approval. Add to this the fact that the officer could sign for his own mail without other censorship except the possibility that the letter might be read at the base port, and censorship became another grievance to the enlisted man.

Finally, the greatest factor in morale, good or bad, was that intangible but very real entity, military discipline. The American boy hates to be under authority; to ask for leave to speak to his captain; to request permission to go for a few hours' leave after his day's duties are over; to address an officer in the third person: "Is the captain feeling well this morning, sir?" Most American officers were human enough, with little of the class feeling of the British army. For that reason the soldier rarely hated his own officers, and often was heard to boast of "my lieutenant" or "my captain." The soldier merely hated authority in general, as represented largely by the necessity to salute any unknown officer whom he might meet. He never understood the lectures about the manliness of saluting or its military necessity; he knew only that it was the sign of authority, to which he was subjected.

Perhaps that is the root of the whole matter of morale. A good soldier at the rear was the man who sank his personality and became a unit in the squad. If too strongly defined an individual, he was a marked man; he became company clerk or kitchen police, according to his previous education. The good soldier was the one who acted automatically on receipt of orders, who saluted, said "Yes, sir," turned on his heel and seemed at once to be very busy. Even if he had been an executive or a lawyer in civil life, the constant drill made an automaton of the enlisted man; he sank back into the mind of the crowd, adopted the usual opinions in the usual words, and lost for the time being his personality. Drill made for automatic physical reactions to a certain set of commands and the temporary cessation of thought. In close-order drill Tom Smith submerged his personality and became "Number Three in the rear rank." He learned to swing about at the proper moment, following the man ahead of him, to respond instantly to the word of command without hesitating for its meaning, to stand and march and salute and obey. That was good for the rear, but at the front we needed Tom Smith again, and he might forget his place in the line, rush forward on his own initiative and become a hero. The finest acts were those of individuals acting without orders, the private forming a stretcher party of volunteers to go out for the wounded, the corporal reforming the platoon when all the sergeants were disabled and leading them forward. Then in the long period after the war Tom Smith had to be lost, for Number Three in the rear ranks was needed again.

The soldier lived in utter ignorance, not only of general events in the world and the army, but even of the things which would affect himself most closely. The enlisted man never knew a day in advance when he would be transferred to a different post or a different duty, when he would be promoted or degraded in rank, when he was to attack the enemy or retire for a rest. Even the things he saw became distorted. A doughboy remarked to me just before the battle of the Selle River, "We're held up by a little stream twenty feet wide, with Jerry on top of the railroad embankment on the other side. If we can just get across that river and up that embankment, we'll end the war right there." Of course, our success three days later did not end the war; it was only part of a tremendous program which the private soldier did not envisage at all. The attack on the Selle River was but one of a half-dozen actions carried on simultaneously in Flanders, on the Scheld, at Rheims, in the Argonne and on the Meuse. Our attack was made easier because of these others, and they in turn were successful because of us. The three hundred miles of battle-line were all one, and only the broadest possible view could give any idea at all of the truth.

The officer, especially when on the staff, saw things in relation, but the soldier had to work in the dark. He never did understand the rules of the great game he was playing. Tactics were nothing to him. He knew only what it meant to march with a heavy pack all night, to rest in the damp cold of dawn when he was too weary to rest at all, to advance under fire and to dig in again and yet again. Much as he might later on revel in the raw heroism of it all, this arduous labor, blind-folded, left him a prey to doubt and rumor at the time. Rumors were one of the few foes of morale which persisted at both front and rear, because they were the product of ignorance and in both places ignorance persisted. No man can be quite steady in his duty when his mind is distracted by the countless rumors of army life. So far as we had information to dispense, we were building up morale, even when the facts were not reassuring. Rumors about going home, being the most desirable, were the greatest menace of all. Men would come back from the hospital with half-healed wounds because the rumor said we were going home at once, and they wanted to go along. Men would take unofficial leave to see Paris before they died, just because the latest rumor had it that we were not to leave for another month. Every such disappointment or lapse of duty made the next rumor more dangerous and wider spread.

The morale of the overseas forces described a slow

downward curve from the high point at the armistice until the news that the particular unit was going home, when it took an immediate upward bound. During the downward trend of the curve, the men grew to hate the army. The definite elements which they naturally resented were emphasized and exaggerated, although that was hardly necessary. At the same time, they felt immense pride in their own achievements, and a thorough contempt for "joy-riders," as they termed the civilian travelers through France, the official investigators or representatives of civilian organizations, who witnessed the trenches as if on a sight-seeing party. This pride in their actual accomplishments, combined with resentment at the military subversion of ordinary civilian standards of life and manhood, was characteristic of the best minds in the ranks.

The military system is of necessity heteronomous, while democracy must be autonomous. The very virtues of self-reliance, independence, responsibility, which we most emphasize in civil life, were the ones most actively discouraged among enlisted men. At the same time, the moral influences put upon them were those of compulsion and restraint. The régime for officers was radically different; it demanded responsibility and removed much of the restraint. Hence the tendency of the army system was to produce officers with adequate mental processes and soldiers with automatic obedience to any kind of orders. The result, not difficult to foresee, was that the officers had far better minds but far poorer morals than the enlisted men. The officer was responsible for himself; the enlisted man had a number of superiors responsible for him. As a consequence the officer used his mind, the soldier stopped using his. On the other hand, the officer often abused his larger liberty, so that some of the officers of the A. E. F. were notorious for their loose living on the boulevards of Paris and other towns and brought shame upon their more decent comrades and the cause for which they fought.

The conspicuous difference was not the result of differences in the men themselves, for we had no castes in the American army. Officers and men came from the same stock and from every group. It was the direct consequence of the different type of discipline and control to which they were subjected. The best officers and the best men surmounted it; the worst yielded; the average were affected more or less.

Obviously, morale was a loose general term for many actual conditions. It meant one thing at the front, another thing at the rear. It included morals, although sometimes a high state of morale could exist together with many lapses from the moral code. It summed up the general state of mind of the troops at any time with regard to the special purpose for which the troops were just then intended. A study of morale gave insight into many related factors, including that of morality. The young man, as we saw him in the army, had a morality of his own, related closely to sport and business, but to neither law nor religion. It is a moral standard—we cannot possibly mistake that— the young man is not in his own mind immoral. But it is a standard which makes much of friendship,

loyalty, fair play, something of honesty, nothing of
the special code which we usually call "morality."
It allowed much laxity in sexual relations; it laid
no stress at all on obedience to military regulations;
it had hardly such a word as "duty." Religion to
the soldier meant habit, or sentiment, or fear, or
longing; it did not mean a code of morals. The
attempt to build up a moral standard on a basis
of duty to one's country or to one's self was
largely inadequate. Courage the soldier recognized,
and sincerity and self-sacrifice; he did not know
much of duty. This fact was both the cause and the
result of military discipline, which made duty an
external matter of obedience to a million trivial and
arbitrary rules, rather than to a few definite and outstanding principles. The young man has a morality of his own in civil life; he had a slightly different,
but related morality in the army. It was not the
conventional morality of society, which rests upon
the historical standards of the middle-aged. It was
a type of morality which we must learn to recognize
and understand for both his benefit and that of society as a whole.

CHAPTER XIII

THE MORAL GAIN AND LOSS OF THE SOLDIER

THE military system, as I have tried to bring out in the last chapter, had a definite and profound influence on the life and thought of the individual soldier. It was so radically different from civilian life that this influence became all the more striking through contrast. The young man has certain moral standards and habits in civil life, some of which became intensified, while others altered in the army. The millions of young men who went through the military régime during the war have brought this influence back into civilian life with them, even though it is attenuated by enviroment and although they have largely returned to their former, pre-military habits. War and danger brought out certain characteristics and occasioned others. These new reactions of character were not, as the pacifists would have it, all bad; neither were they all good, as was generally proclaimed in patriotic fashion while the war was going on. Some influences were good and some were bad, while almost every man in the service would necessarily respond to both kinds. The military system itself caused or brought to light certain good and bad traits which appeared clearly enough in the average soldier after he had been in the army even a few months. It may be worth while to develop some of these at a little length, not scientifically nor psychologically, but simply and directly as they strike the soldier himself.

We saw at the front, as the experience of other armies had indicated, that the average man has in him the stuff of which heroes are made. Not merely the farmer or backwoodsman, but the men who followed prosaic city occupations, were ready to sacrifice themselves for their comrades and their country. The barber and the shipping clerk were as frequent winners of the D. S. C. as any others in our huge heterogeneous army. Heroism was evoked by the need, by the fact that it was the expected response, the response of thousands of others. The crowd mind produced heroism out of the most unexpected material. War created some of the heroism which we saw; it merely evoked some which was already latent, ready for the call. The stretcher-bearer, exposing himself to the severest fire to carry his precious burden to safety; the battalion runner, bearing his message through the barrage and then coming back again to bring the answer; the machine gunner, carrying his heavy weapon on his back to an advanced position where he could establish it effectively; the infantryman, advancing against machine-gun fire, or digging in under attack from heavy artillery or aëroplanes; the engineer, digging away debris or laying bridges in plain sight of the enemy, with his rifle laid near by to use in case of an attack—I might enumerate hundreds of such duties in which courage, loyalty, and endurance were exhibited by men who performed exceptional acts of bravery and devotion, volunteering for difficult service or carrying on in the face of overwhelming

odds. All soldiers were afraid, but in the performance of their duty practically all soldiers learned to
overcome fear and attend to their jobs in the face
of every obstacle and every danger.

We felt that travel, with its attendant contact
with other customs, language and people, would
broaden our soldiers mentally and tend to break
down the provincialism which has been often noticed
in America, as well as in many other countries.
Only a small minority of our men were equipped,
either in knowledge or in attitude, to take advantage
of the opportunities offered. Museums meant comparatively little to them, mediæval cathedrals not
much more, Roman walls or ruins nothing at all.
Scenery did not mean as much as some of us thought
it should, forgetting that scenery looks entirely different to a man who rides past it and another who
walks through it. Altogether, knowledge of France,
England and Germany made, on the whole, not for
a greater appreciation of foreign lands, but instead
for a great appreciation of America.

The fact is that the boys grew homesick. Most
of them were only boys in years, and practically
all of them were reduced to the boyish level of
thought by the general irresponsibility, thought-
lessness, and dependency of army life. They were
like boys in a military school, very often, rather than
men engaged in the grim business of modern war.
To these boys absence from home brought a higher
appreciation of home. This was often a true evalua-
tion, in the face of previous neglect and under-
estimation; sometimes it may have been a senti-
mentalizing of a home that had never really meant
very much. But in the danger, the monotony, and

the distance, the soldiers grew to higher appreciation of their own homes and their home-land as
well.

Their complaints were often ridiculous enough.
They objected to the backwardness, the lack of sani-
tation, the absence of bathing facilities in the French
villages. These were true enough, as far as they
went, although I know personally that they can be
matched in many details even in prosperous and en-
lightened America. They objected to the French
climate, with the damp cold of its winters, not caring to remember that certain parts of our own
Pacific coast suffer from a rainy season, too. This
complaint becomes still more valueless when we
remember how the boys grumbled about the heat
of the Texas border, in fact, how soldiers not in
action will always find a source of complaint in the
weather, whatever kind of weather it may be. As
General O'Ryan remarked in his famous definition
of a soldier, "A soldier is a man who always wants
to be somewhere else than where he is." This
restlessness accounts for some of the complaints
which we are apt to take a bit too seriously. A
more real complaint was the language difficulty.
Soldier French was a wonderful thing, consisting
of the names of all ordinary things to eat and
drink, together with a few common expressions, such
as "toute de suite" (always pronounced "toot
sweet"), and "combien." This prevented easy
communication, even with such French people as
were encountered. Few of the soldiers had any opportunity to use even their little French on respectable, middle-class French families, especially not on
young men or girls. All these grievances, real and

fancied, put the soldier out of ease in France and made him appreciate America so much the better. The sacrifices they were making for America, the service they were rendering her, united with the home-sickness of a stranger in a strange land to increase the devotion and respect of Americans for America.

I need not refer especially to the rather mixed gain in religious attitude, as I have already devoted a chapter to that subject. I must, however, repeat one point I mentioned there, the meaning of physical sacrifice as these men saw it and practised it in the army. It was the outcome of their courage, their dash, their enthusiasm, that when the time of stress came ordinary men offered their lives for their friends and their country. The soldier at the front equaled or exceeded the forgetfulness of self of the fireman or the life-saver in time of peace. This lesson of self-forgetfulness, of self-sacrifice, was one of the great impressions made by the war upon the best men it influenced, and one which touched in its way even the most thoughtless and careless of all the soldiers who had their hour at the front.

This brought out the group solidarity of the American army in stronger relief. The fine thing about morale at the front, as I have outlined it, was the mutual confidence which it called out in every breast. The pride in his own company, his regiment, his division, in the American army as a whole, which held a man to his duty under fire and impelled him to resist the almost overwhelming influence of a sudden attack of panic, made for loyalty at the rear as well and formed one basis for the whole-hearted return of the young men into civilian society after the war. Pride in one's division meant also pride in one's state; pride in the United States Army meant pride in the United States. Self-sacrifice, devotion, heroism,—all these were profound lessons for any man, young or old, a lesson which American democracy can profitably utilize in the daily humdrum of American life.

It was surprising how constantly our expectations were disappointed by the actual facts of the men in the service. Most books and articles since the war and all of those before the war were written on a theoretical basis, and every one approached the facts with a theoretical view. But the theory was proved wrong in so many instances that I am making the present study entirely empirical, leaving theory out altogether as more of a pitfall than an advantage. For one thing, I had expected war to exert a directly brutalizing influence on the soldier. This was never evident at all except in the actual stress of battle when killing was a daily necessity, and human life, although the most valuable asset of the contending forces, was still held cheaply enough to be used up at a terrific rate. Men could not stop there to pity every corpse; they had to save their own lives and at the same time to win the war. But the effect wore off quickly; probably it left no result at all except on men with a previous tendency to brutality or crime. I remember the thrill of horror which went through Le Mans and the entire A. E. F. in April 1919, when a railroad accident occurred near our post and a group of soldiers and sailors on furlough were injured, some of them fatally. We forgot all about the fact that these men had risked death in entering the service, that the few of them in this accident were the smallest fraction of a day's toll at the front if the war had continued. We melted in sympathy, and the French population of Le Mans did the same.

The men were not brutalized, contrary to expectation. Human life was held cheaply under exceptional circumstances and evidently the men felt that they were exceptional. But the men did become accustomed to the use of firearms, and those already brutalized were given the knowledge and the means for crimes of violence. The carelessness with which men used and flung about all kinds of deadly weapons shocked those of us with a sense of responsibility; it was part of their boyish heedlessness in the midst of the fierce game they were playing. They threw their discarded rifles in a heap by the first-aid post when they went back to hospital; they even played catch with hand-grenades, sometimes with most serious results. Once I met a pair of Australians out hunting rabbits with their high-powered rifles, in a place where hundreds of men were passing hourly by the much-traveled road. When I remonstrated with them, they only replied, "Oh, well, we haven't anything else to do. And we know how to shoot without hurting anybody."

But with all these real character acquisitions on the part of the men in the service, and with the lack of that brutalizing which many theorists had feared, at the same time certain moral losses were occasioned by the military system. I shall not enter into the question of sexual morality here, partly because I have discussed it in the previous chapter, and partly because it was not distinctly the product of the army. The sexual standards of the young men in the army were much the same as those of young men everywhere, with some modifications through discipline. But to the man who has served in any army at any time, the outstanding moral weakness of the soldier is his entire disregard of the rights of property. The sense of property, so strong in civilian life, which is implanted so carefully into the little child, seems lost in the first month of a man's army life. One brigade headquarters I knew in France was established in a fine château, with large grounds surrounded by a high wooden fence. At the same time, the men of the nearest unit were living in barns and attics, with no light or heat of any kind in their quarters. The result was that the fence disappeared, little by little. Nobody ever saw the culprits, but I had reliable information that the men billeted in that village had all the heat they needed. When we left the area, about half the fence was gone, and I have little doubt it vanished entirely during the occupancy of the next division.

I can still hear the indignation of the driver of my "tin Lizzie" when the precious lamps were stolen out of our car and we had to drive home ten miles in the dark. Of course, lamps were scarce, having to be shipped from the States, and the thief undoubtedly drove an army car like ours. But a few days later after a visit to the city my driver reported back in triumph—he had found another machine parked in a side street and "salvaged" the lights. I tried to make him return them, but for once he proved insubordinate. It was only another army car; the other fellow had probably got them the same way; he could not identify the car, anyway. Then came the finishing stroke when we tried the lights and found them burned out! The other driver had left them in as a blind. My driver felt a sense of personal injury, as though he had been directly cheated in a legitimate business deal. And practically any soldier would have agreed with him.

The men "found" whatever they needed if it was not issued to them properly, because property had no meaning to them in the army. They owned nothing whatever; even their clothes, food and lodging belonged to Uncle Sam. When their clothes wore out, they were replaced; when the company's weekly supply of food was eaten up, more was forthcoming. Rifles fallen into disrepair were exchanged for good ones; shoes were sent to the salvage depot to be repaired and then issued to another man. Equipment lost at the front or in the hospital was reissued without question. Therefore the enlisted man felt a community sense of ownership rather than a personal one. At the same time, he was constantly in need of one thing or another. He needed fire wood, as in the incident of the fence, or automobile supplies, as with my driver. The legend even goes that the Australians, famous in their ability to care for their own units, have been known to take an entire field kitchen, with the food still cooking, from a British unit and make a successful escape. I know that I have personally seen a British colonial soldier in a village near the front taking a large mirror with a gilt frame out of a dwelling house and making off toward his quarters. "What are you doing with that?" I asked him.

"Oh, I think we can use it," was his unembarrassed answer.

The soldier learned to disregard law, just as he learned to disregard property. Discipline meant obedience to constant minute surveillance. It meant getting up at reveille, rolling his blankets in just such a way, reporting at roll call, lining up for mess, working at whatever menial tasks he might be detailed to do by the sergeant, asking for a pass when he wanted to go to the nearest city, submitting his mail to censorship, getting a day off for sickness only after lining up for "sick call," and finally going to bed at night as soon as the bugle sounded "taps." These men were not trained soldiers, accustomed to such a system; they were healthy American boys in whom this constant subjection to external control meant the immediate seeds of revolt. Autonomy meant then the evasion of the law. A man could assert his individuality only in such ways as going absent without leave, wearing a serge uniform (not regulation for private soldiers), or gambling away his last month's scanty pay. Add to this his constant contact with officers, who, if they had to bear a heavy burden of responsibility and were forced to pay for all the things the enlisted man received for nothing, still were not subject to many of the restrictions which he found most galling. The test of manly independence came to be simply "getting away with it." If a man was caught in an infraction of the rules he had to take his punishment; if he was not detected or not convicted he was a successful soldier. This applied, for example, to a trip to Paris, the golden dream of every American soldier. For a long time this was strictly forbidden, although later three-day leaves to Paris were allowed to a certain number of men. Yet thousands of Americans saw the lovely and forbidden city unofficially. They got leave to Versailles, and rode into Paris daily by street car. They took the wrong train, ostensibly by accident, and had to change trains at Paris, dropping out of sight for a day or two meanwhile. They borrowed the travel orders of other men and used them over, risking detection. Neither the extreme harshness of the Paris military police nor the menace of their own angry captains could keep them from the enticing adventure. It was their boyishness, combined with their lack of respect for the law itself, that led them into such devious modes of disobedience. "If you know how, you can get away with murder," was the usual apology—further excuse was not needed.

Among officers a similar tendency showed itself in a different way. The officer was not limited in the most petty ways which irritated the men, although he also could not take a trip to Paris without proper travel orders and could not absent himself from duty without special permission. But the officer likewise grew to disregard the law essentially, even while he obeyed it most carefully in its minutiæ. An officer was bound by his signature on written documents. A request coming from the sergeant had to be endorsed by the lieutenant, with his reasons if he did not favor granting it. It would then pass on to the captain, the major, the colonel, and if necessary also the brigadier and the major general. Having passed through military channels for its consideration, it came back again by the same route until it reached the originator. This system made at once for diffusion of responsibility, or, to use the familiar army term, "passing the buck." The first man who approved the request had no responsibility, as it was approved likewise by his superiors; the later endorsers had none, as they had signed it on his recommendation, assuming his knowledge of the facts. Nobody could be held responsible and every one was careful to evade responsibility wherever he could. Naturally, this made for endless delays, for complications interminable when a previous order had to be rescinded for any reasons whatever, for evasion in case of difficulty or doubt. It meant fundamentally the disregard of law, expressed by the soldier in disobedience and by the officer in evasion.

The military régime likewise tended to break down habits of regular industry. During the war there was the alternation of short periods of intense and exhausting activity at the front and longer ones of as complete rest as the men could obtain at the rear. It was a reversion to the life of the savage, busy by spells at hunting or war, with rest and languor between. The entire exhaustion, physical and mental, after a "spell in the trenches" demanded complete relaxation afterward, while there was always a little necessary work in the way of drill, reëquipment and inspection. After the war was over, the drill went on in still larger doses but without the incentive of returning to the trenches again afterward. This alternation of work and rest together with the general rebellion against routine, broke down the habit of consistent work which is built up with such effort and such inducements in civil life. Boys do not want to work until they are taught to do so and given inducements in the form of money and the things money will buy. But the soldiers, so boyish in their life and their feelings, had few such inducements given them. Their universal experience after leaving the army was that it took a tremendous effort of will to return to the routine and responsibility of a civilian occupation.

Exceptions existed, of course, to every generalization in this chapter, as they do to any generalization of any kind. But the exceptions speedily lifted themselves out of the ranks by promotion, and were therefore covered by the different influences on the officers and the higher ranks of non-commissioned officers. And I feel that even these exceptional men who retained their respect for law and property, their habits of regular industry, did so only in comparison with the general break-down, that even they felt a certain loosening of the standards which they had possessed in civilian life.

Army life developed a new series of moral values and moral reactions. It brought out virtues which were latent or non-existent in civil life; it reduced others to impotence. It produced love of country, of home, and of God; it brought forth courage, loyalty, self-sacrifice, the extreme of heroism, in such numbers and such variety that they seemed commonplace. It did not brutalize any who were not very ready for such a process. But at the same time, it destroyed the citizen's respect for law and order, his respect for property, his habit of hard and persistent work. It made him, for the time being, a lazy hero; a jovial, careless, and lovable lawbreaker. It brought out exactly the qualities which are least necessary in civil life, and injured those most necessary; it took the student, the workingman, the farmer, and made of him the doughboy. Army life was opposed directly to the whole tenor of democracy, the régime where men control themselves, where they work through ambition and desire for success, and where they strive to accumulate property of their own, at the same time respecting the law and the property of others. Army life meant a break in the lives of millions of young Americans, an interruption of the steady development of their characters and habits, a reversal of their tendencies and a postponement of their ambitions.

I feel that it is a great evidence of the essential soundness of American manhood that these millions have returned to civil life, in most cases to their former circles and their former occupations, with so little difficulty. Society helped them at the moment by the splendid reception home, by the plaudits, the speeches, and the parades. It helped them also to obtain positions and then left them to find themselves. Fortunately, after a brief transition most of them did find themselves, and the ex-soldiers to-day are back in every type of work as before. The former captain may sell you a suit; the holder of a D. S. C. may wait on you at the restaurant. They have overcome the restlessness, the carelessness, the thrill; they are civilians again. But here and there the seeds fell on different soil; here and there a former soldier has not found himself again. We see him most often among the wounded and gassed, who cannot fit into industry so easily, and whose sufferings have often affected their mentality and always their point of view. America has wasted criminally precious years of these young ruined lives, in not bringing to them instantly the full care and service of a grateful nation. On the other hand, industry has made little effort to absorb our soldiers; I have seen men with trades selling fruit from push-carts because there was no other work at hand. I have seen a jobless boy, honestly trying to make a little money by selling trinkets in the street and driven away by a patriotic store-keeper, who felt that he had done his duty by buying Liberty Bonds and need not bother about the man who had fought his battles for him. The soldier who cannot return to civil life is a rare exception, but he is an exception caused in an unstable youth by our military or our industrial system. Our nation, which profited by that army, must remember for good every weakest individual whose sweat and blood poured forth to make that army great.

CHAPTER XIV

THE JEWISH SOLDIER AND JUDAISM

DURING the war we were so stunned by its suddenness and vastness that we felt it would shatter all former systems of philosophy, that men would need a new philosophy of life after the war, just as they did after the Renaissance or the epoch-making discoveries of Darwin. This opinion, natural enough at the time, was certainly exaggerated. The war did not shatter all ideals; it did not create any new ones except the wave of spiritualism at present so wide-spread. But it did shift emphases, exposed the hollowness of many easy beliefs, and implanted new ideas in minds which otherwise might not have been ready for them. The soldier really presents the typical reaction to the war, while the civilian shows a milder type of influence and a smaller degree of change. The revaluation of values which is really demanded to-day is nothing so fundamental as we thought at the time. It is chiefly psychological, that we shall understand what is in the mind of the soldier, and by that means reach an understanding of the effect of the war on society as a whole. The world contains in diluted form those same influences which show so distinctly on these young men. The problem of evil is neither greater nor less than it was before the war; the problem of life and death is no dif-

ferent; the problem of conduct has not changed.
But certain phases of each of these problems have
come very strongly to the attention of the world;
some of them have been branded into the consciousness of the soldier. Just as the soldier has a viewpoint toward American ideals, which America would
do well to heed in working out her programs for the
era after the war, so the Jewish soldier has his own
viewpoint toward Judaism, which all who are interested in our people and our religion need to
understand and utilize for the best development of
our religious programs in the days that are just
ahead.

It is hard to call the soldier a progressive in
religion when he had so few theories about the
matter. But he was certainly not a traditionalist.
Religious ideas and practices had to satisfy his immediate needs or they had no meaning to him at
all. This covered all cant words, all ready-made
formulas, whether as ancient as the Talmud or as
comparatively recent as reform Judaism. The answer of a twelfth century Jew of Spain or a nine-
teenth century Jew of Germany were on an equal-
ity to him; if either solved the problems of a young
American at war it was acceptable. The soldier
was willing to accept old answers to new questions
if they were cogent; on the other hand, he was quite
as willing to consider a new and revolutionary
theory. He possessed that rare attribute, the open
mind; on the narrow but keen basis of his own mental
experience he grasped and estimated soundly the
new ideas and the old.

The soldier enjoyed ceremonies that reminded him
of home and childhood, but he regarded them largely

as pleasant memories. However deep a meaning
the symbols might possess, the soldier had not the
background to grasp it. The symbols did not stand
for enough to solve the problems of his immediate
life. In the same way, theological concepts, however liberal, meant nothing to him practically. The
liberal theology of reform Judaism might have appealed to the mass of the Jewish soldiers if they
had been interested in it and had made an effort
to understand it. As it was, liberalism in theology
meant exactly nothing to them. They were not interested in theological problems; they did not care
what one's opinion might be about the literal inspiration of the Bible or about the coming of the
Messiah. The liberalism which expressed itself constantly among the soldiers, and which they brought
back with them into civil life, was different from
all this. Granting your liberalism or your con-
servatism in regard to beliefs and ceremonies, the
soldier wanted to know your attitude toward other
human beings. The liberalism he wanted was social
and humanitarian. On this plane he had his being.
This was the type of problem which interested him
and which he could understand. The soldier felt
too often that the churches and synagogues were
dominated by capital, by a narrow social class which
discriminated against him. Among Jewish soldiers,
many felt that the religious ideas they might accept
were expressed in rich reform temples, where they
themselves would not be acceptable or would not
feel at home. On the other hand, they did not feel
at home in the little orthodox synagogues where
their fathers offered up their daily prayers. They
did not understand the Hebrew ritual uttered there,

nor the devotional attitude which was there expressed.

But all this is not reaching directly the synagogue
itself. The young men, the former soldiers, are not
the trustees of our temples and synagogues; they
are not a majority of our members; they are not
often to be found in the pews, where we might see
their response to a particular service or a particular
sermon. If we are not very careful, the churches
and synagogues will lose entirely the inspiration of
their youthful vigor and find themselves tied entirely to the generation which has passed into middle
age and is becoming old. We must call to the
young men in the voice of youth, with the viewpoint and on the plane which they understand and
on which they may respond. That means that we
must be willing to accept new conclusions to new
problems if these conclusions seem to fit the new
times'. That means also that we must have an
aggressive attitude toward social and economic
problems. This alone can make liberalism religious and make religion concrete, applicable to
the needs of the latest era, the era after the world
war. Without it, religion will remain moribund,
liberalism irreligious. Religious bodies must give
an equal hearing to both the conservative and the
radical, must show a definite platform of religious
and moral work on which the two can unite. That
was done during the war. All groups in American
Jewry, orthodox, conservative and reform, were associated in the Jewish Welfare Board and still work
together on the Joint Distribution Committee for
the relief of Jewish war sufferers. All groups in
American life, Jew and non-Jew alike, met and

worked together in the United War Work campaign, to care for the soldiers in our emergency. But the young men, no longer soldiers, need us as badly now, while we, the churches and the synagogues, need them more than ever, with their new experience and their newfound manhood. What they need and what we need, too, is that we learn to coöperate on a common platform of action for their benefit now. If we want them, if we want to be at one with them, we must have a social program, a liberal attitude to life and especially to its most immediate economic problems, a willingness to sink differences of opinion that we may meet for practical effort and genuine progress.

The boys in the service became largely socialized through the tremendous, constant work of the welfare agencies. They felt the value of the Y. M. C. A. or other welfare hut, not only for the entertainments, dances and canteen, but just as much as a center for the soldier community, a place to write, to read, to play games, to meet their friends. Since their return they have turned to such institutions as the Y. M. C. A., the Y. M. H. A. and the rest, to find the club life, the community spirit, which they had in the welfare hut in camp or city at home and abroad. This need of the young men for a social center and a social life is a common need of all America. Every village needs a social center to further its growth into a finer culture and a more united citizenship. Every Jewish community large enough to have a little social life of its own needs a community center where that life can flourish and be guided in desirable and constructive channels. The expansion of the Jewish Welfare

Board to join and assist the activities of the National Council of Young Men's Hebrew and Kindred Associations is a logical one, growing out of the similar needs of the same young men in war and peace. The furtherance of social centers for Jewish communities, for other groups of citizens who possess a common heritage or common background, and for a whole town where the town is not too large, is a piece of work in which the soldiers will participate and which their very existence among us should suggest to the rest of the community. The return of the soldier may assist us more than we expect in socializing the Jewish community. The social spirit we once showed in his behalf, the social education we gave him while in the service, will return to benefit us all if we convert the two into Jewish social life. Such a socializing will cut across congregational or sectional lines, across lines of birth and wealth, and unite the Jewish community in America, just as the same process will eventually, if carried far enough, weld together all the divergent social forces of America itself.

The need for personal religion at the front was a temporary need, or rather a temporary expression of a universal human yearning. It is now almost forgotten by the boys themselves, certainly by the church and the synagogue. Beside the liberal and the social demands of the day, there exists this mystical longing to be sure of God, to know for a certainty that He will protect His dear ones. This universal and eternal need was felt for the time by our men in immediate danger, in thankfulness, in mourning. Having discovered it once, they still feel it when the occasion

comes. Here, however, there seems little likelihood
of their contribution being accepted. The union of
the social and mystical elements, even at different
times and for different occasions, seems more than
any human institution can accomplish. If the soldier, in tune with the urge of the age, demands a
social and a liberal response from the synagogue,
he may get it in a large number of cases. The
mystical element he will not ask for, and his inarticulate mood, now hardly evident, will certainly
evoke no response.

One thing certainly the young men feel, which
American Judaism is accepting from them. While
the young Jew is wholly sympathetic to Zionism, he
hardly ever feels that Zionism is the center or the
conclusion of the Jewish problem. Zionism, as a
movement, has brought to fruition much of the
latent love of the young Jew for his people and
his religion. But the Jewish soldier, or the same
boy as a civilian, is not interested chiefly in solving
the economic or the cultural problems of Palestine.
He responds also to the similar problems among the
Jews of America. Zionism is not enough for him;
he must have Judaism as well. He and all
of us are compelled to confront the spiritual and
moral problems of the new world after the war.

The young man does not know, and the synagogue
does not always show him, that the very things
he demands most urgently are inherent in Judaism,
especially in those great prophets whose words still
ring forth with a youthful fervor. The unfaltering
search for new truth, the recognition of the poor
and the weak, the unity of all groups in the community, the triumphant search for God and finding

of God—all these the young Jew wants and the prophets have given us. This aspect of the problem, then, becomes one of leadership, to interpret our Judaism in terms which express the life of the new day and to show the young men that their dearest longings are part of the ancient Jewish heritage. The antiquity of the prophetic summons is no disadvantage to the young men if it answers their personal need. It is of the greatest advantage to the synagogue in responding to the call of the great days after the war. Those ancient responses to the errors and crimes of mobs and despots in the Orient contain principles whose vitality is not impaired by the passage of time. It needs but the skill and the courage to apply them again, as in prophetic times, to the western world in the twentieth century.

War gave the world a new angle of vision on life and death, on good and bad. The deepest impress of this new viewpoint is on those men who were themselves at the front, who underwent the most extreme phase of it in their own persons, but some traces have spread throughout the entire western civilization. America must realize it as Europe does; Judaism and Christianity alike are entering, for good or bad, a new period. The world has changed in some respects; we who see the world have changed far more. In facing the future, with its political, its social, its moral problems, we need a new fullness of insight into the young men whose lives have changed and whose souls expanded overnight, even though they remain in externals the boys they were. We need a new intellectual content, covering not only the new map of Europe and Asia, but also the new ideas and ideals which swept the

world for a time, as though they were to be eternal.
Above all, we must have complete honesty in facing
the thrilling challenge of the immediate future.   We
do not need a new form of Judaism any more than
we need a new type of government in America.
We are confronted by the demand to adapt Americanism and Judaism to the changing demands of a
changing era, to find among the temporary and
evanescent elements in both those things which have
permanent usefulness for any demand and any era.
We need ideals of the past, indeed, but only such
ideals as have survived the past, as apply fully to
the present, as will aid in building up a future of
promise and achievement for the Jew.   Judaism is
on trial to-day.   If we answer the need of the young
man, he will be the loyal, active Jew for to-day and
to-morrow.   If we ignore him, whether through uncertainty, ignorance or pride, he will not come to
us and we shall not be going after him.   Judaism
needs the young man; it needs equally his great
ideals, social and mystical as well.   The test will result in a finer and more effective faith only if
we respond to it bravely and honestly, in the very
spirit of the soldier himself.

CHAPTER XV

THE JEWISH SOLDIER AND ANTI-SEMITISM

DURING the war we felt that prejudice between men of different groups and different faiths was lessening day by day, that our common enthusiasm in our common cause had brought Catholics, Protestants and Jews nearer together on a basis of their ardent Americanism. Especially we who were at the front felt this in the first flush of our coöperation, our mutual interest and our mutual helpfulness. After you have stood beside a man in the stress of front-line work, have shared a blanket with him, have seen him suffer like a hero or die like a martyr, his origin, his family and his faith become less important than the manhood of the man himself. More than once I have said, talking to soldier audiences of Jewish or of mixed faith: "After this war no man can knowingly call the Jew a coward again. If you ever hear such a statement, you can be sure that our detractor is not an honest bigot, as may have been the case in the past; he is either ignorant or malicious."

We knew that and our comrades knew it. The men at the front knew very little about the whole-hearted participation of every section of our vast population, Jew and non-Jew together, in the campaigns for production, Liberty Bonds, the United War Work campaign, and all the rest. That record is a permanent one and is known to every man who did his duty in "the rear lines" back in the United States during the war. But those who served overseas know the record the Jew made for himself at the front, his promotions, his decorations, his woundings and his deaths. They know that differences of religion and race counted not at all in the American army, that our heroes and our effective, able soldiers came from all religions and all races. With what high hopes we entered the war; with what fine fervor we saw it end! We felt that our efforts had insured something more of liberty for the oppressed of all the world, for Czech and Armenian, Alsatian and Belgian, Pole and Jew.

Perhaps the greatest disappointment of all to the fighters and the sufferers has been the survival and the occasional revival of the old hatreds in a more intense form. I am thinking of the many national and group hatreds and antagonisms which have tormented the world in the last years, and especially of one of them, that against the Jews. The oppression of the autocratic régime of the Czar has been carried on by the free nation of Poland; the pogroms of the Black Hundred have been revived in the Ukraine, where the slaughter of war was doubled by the slaughter of peace. Hungary has seen its "white terror," where Jews were murdered as Bolshevists and Bolshevists as Jews. Austria and Germany have seen a strengthening of the political anti-Semitism of pre-war times, here blaming the Jews for beginning the war, and there for ending it. Finally the movement has been carried over into the freest and most intelligent of nations, and some apologists for it have appeared even in England and America. Here the Anti-Semites can work by neither political nor legal means, but through a campaign of slander they strive to weaken the morale of the Jew and injure his standing before the mass of his fellow citizens.

I shall not turn aside to deal, even for a moment, with the mass of accusations against the Jew, trivial or grave as the case may be. They have been adequately answered by Jew and non-Jew, especially in the address on ''The 'Protocols,' Bolshevism and the Jews,'' by ten national organizations of American Jews on December 1, 1920, and the subsequent protests against anti-Semitism by a distinguished group of non-Jewish Americans, notably President Woodrow Wilson, former President William Howard Taft and William Cardinal O'Connell. The only one of these accusations with which I can properly deal in this place, and one on which my fellow-soldiers will agree with me in every detail, is the revival of the ancient slander against the patriotism and courage of the Jew. We are reading, not for the first time in history, but for almost the first time in the *English* language, that the Jews are not patriots in their respective nations, that they all have a super-national allegiance to a Jewish international conspiracy, that their real loyalty is to this other group within and above the state, even to the extent of treachery or anarchy against their own governments. We feel the disgrace, the pathos of such a charge just after the war when Jews died with non-Jews that America might be safe, at a time when Jews even more than non-Jews are enduring the dread aftermath of war, the famine, the poverty

and the epidemics, in Eastern and Central Europe.
It is the sort of charge which only facts can answer,
the kind of facts which are present in this book,
as in every official or personal story of the war by
men who took a personal part in the war. Prejudice
is too largely the product of those who gained by
the war but did not personally enter the ranks.
The men who know, the men who fought together
and bled together, have a different story.

America has, in fact, too much fairness as well as
too much humanity, to listen to any such movement of partisan hatred or bigotry. I quote the
statement of over a hundred distinguished "citizens
of Gentile birth and Christian faith," referred to
above:

"The loyalty and patriotism of our fellow citizens
of the Jewish faith is equal to that of any part
of our people, and requires no defense at our hands.
From the foundations of this Republic down to
the recent World War, men and women of Jewish
ancestry and faith have taken an honorable part in
building up this great nation and maintaining its
prestige and honor among the nations of the world.
There is not the slightest justification, therefore, for
a campaign of anti-Semitism in this country."

In this connection, we can recall the words written
by Theodore Roosevelt, at that time President, in
1905, on the occasion of the 250th anniversary of
the first landing of Jews in what is now the United
States:

"I am glad to be able to say that while the Jews of
the United States have remained loyal to their faith
and their race traditions, they are engaged in
generous rivalry with their fellow-citizens of other

denominations in advancing the interests of our common country. This is true, not only of the descendants of the early settlers and those of American birth, but of a great and constantly increasing proportion of those who have come to our shores within the last twenty-five years as refugees reduced to the direst straits of penury and misery. In a few years, men and women hitherto utterly unaccustomed to any of the privileges of citizenship have moved mightily upward toward the standard of loyal, self-respecting American citizenship; of that citizenship which not merely insists upon its rights, but also eagerly recognizes its duty to do its full share in the material, social and moral advancement of the nation.''

It would be beside the issue to refer to the Jewish participation in American life during the past, if that also had not been brought up as an accusation. But the records exist, and the facts are conclusive. In the American revolution forty-six Jews fought under George Washington, out of the little Jewish population of about two thousand in the United States at that time. The leading Jews of New York and Newport left those cities because they were patriots and would not carry on their business under British rule. Haim Salomon, the Jewish banker of New York and later of Philadelphia, was among those who rendered the greatest service in financing the infant nation. In the Civil War ten thousand Jewish soldiers of whom we to-day possess the records served in the Union and Confederate armies. Each generation of immigrants has been most eager to learn the English language and American ways, to take advantage to the full of American liberty and opportunity, to make a home for their families in a free land and to help that land maintain its freedom. The World War was for the Jews, as for all Americans, simply the culmination, bringing out most strongly the high lights in American life. Heroes and slackers, loyal and disloyal, showed themselves in their true colors during the war. And the Jew, like all Americans, showed himself in this crisis loyal to America. The Jewish record stands on a par with the best record of any group of American citizens, of any church or any race. Jews of Russia, whose only contact with their native government had fostered hatred and distrust, flocked to the colors in America. Jews of American birth, like all citizens of American birth, did their full duty for their country.

On this point again, my own facts, clear as they are, need not stand alone. I can quote Major General Robert Alexander, who commanded, in the 77th Division, the largest group of Jews in any unit of the American Expeditionary Forces: "I found that Hebrew names on the Honor Roll of the division were fully up to the proportion that they should have been; in other words, the Hebrew boy paid his full share of the price of victory. When the time came for recommendations to go in for marks of distinction which we were able to give, I found there again that the names of the Hebrews were as fully represented on that list as the numbers in the division warranted, by long odds."

To-day the Jewish soldier, no longer a soldier or a hero, but still a Jew and an American, appeals to the American people. Will they suffer such a propaganda, he wonders, such an attack on him and on his brothers who still lie overseas, in their American graves on foreign soil? Will they tolerate for a moment such a venomous and false attack on the defenders of their nation, on any group, small or large, of the boys who rallied to the defense of democracy? In the army overseas we felt that prejudice was a thing of the past, that only in ignorance or malice could the old serpent lift its head again. To-day, with all the newer bitterness, we feel the same. We know that our soldier comrades are loyal still, that America is still America, that as we have once defended her we need not now muster our arguments or records to defend ourselves against her. If the Jew ever needed justification, he surely needs it no longer to-day. The Jewish soldier has once for all made anti-Semitism impossible among the men who served America in arms, and who still in days of quiet continue to serve and save their country.